Nature Guide
SCOTLAND

GARETH FRY

Contents

Cover illustrations:
Top: Capercaillie, Red Deer, Golden Eagle
Centre: Wild Cat, Scottish Primrose, Scotch
Argus
Bottom: Loch Long and the Cobbler
Title page photograph *(page 1):*
Eilean Donan Castle

Edited by Karen Goaman

Series Editor: Karen Goaman

Designed by Anne Sharples

The editor wishes to thank Pauline Khng, who
edited "Places to Visit", and Gareth Fry and Mary
Fane for picture research. The author and
publishers wish to thank the following
organizations for their help: Forestry
Commission, National Trust for Scotland, Nature
Conservancy Council, Royal Society for the
Protection of Birds, Scottish Tourist Board,
Scottish Wildlife Trust.

Most of the illustrations in the section on pages
33–96, Common Species of the Countryside and
Seashore, have been previously published in the
Usborne Spotter's Guides series.

First published in 1981 by
Usborne Publishing Limited
20 Garrick Street, London WC2

Printed and bound in Great Britain by
Fakenham Press Limited, Fakenham, Norfolk

Introduction

Scotland's mosaic of mountain tops, lochs, extensive moorlands, precipitous cliffs, wide estuaries, and ancient pine forests provide a multitude of habitats for wildlife. The country is still relatively unspoilt: a low population and large tracts of land unsuitable for growing crops have allowed certain areas to remain wild.

The variation in climate and geology across Scotland is the basis for the wide-ranging habitats. This is reflected in Scotland's plant life which includes the arctic-alpine species of the mountains — especially abundant in lime-rich areas; plant communities on rocky cliffs resembling garden rockeries; sand dunes with spectacular orchids; and the ancient forests of Scots Pine harbouring special woodland plant species.

Scotland's range of large mammals is the widest in Britain; it includes the rare shy Wild Cat and Pine Marten and the more frequently seen Red Deer and Otter. Scotland's bird life ranges from the thousands of geese, ducks and waders on its estuaries to the magnificent birds of prey hunting over mountain, moor and loch.

The rocky mountainous Highlands are dotted with numerous lochs and smaller "lochans" such as this one.

How to Use this Book

The first section of this book, pages 4-32, illustrated with colour photographs and paintings, describes the habitats that are characteristic of Scotland and the animals and plants special to Scotland. There are colour maps on pages 4-7 showing the main areas in which the habitats occur. Many habitats are closely linked to the geology and climatic conditions of the country: these features are described on pages 8-9.

The middle section of the book, pages 33-96, contains illustrations of over 350 species of animals and plants commonly found in Scotland and over much of Britain. Further details on how to use this section are found on page 33.

The third section of the book, "Places to Visit", found on pages 97-120, consists of a gazetteer containing descriptions of over 200 places of interest. Each region of Scotland has a separate list and a map showing the location of the sites. The places described include specific habitats, nature reserves, nature trails, birdwatching points, and also zoos, wildlife parks, country parks, gardens, museums and study centres. Further details on how to use this section are found on page 97.

Information such as useful addresses, good reference books, hill safety and a full index are found at the end of the book. Use the index to find out whether a species is illustrated — page numbers referring to illustrations appear in bold.

When visiting the countryside, care should be taken to respect the habitats and the wildlife living there. Flowers should not be picked, nesting birds and mammals with young should not be disturbed, and the Country Code, set out on page 121, should always be followed. Some of the problems related to nature conservation in Scotland' are also discussed on page 121.

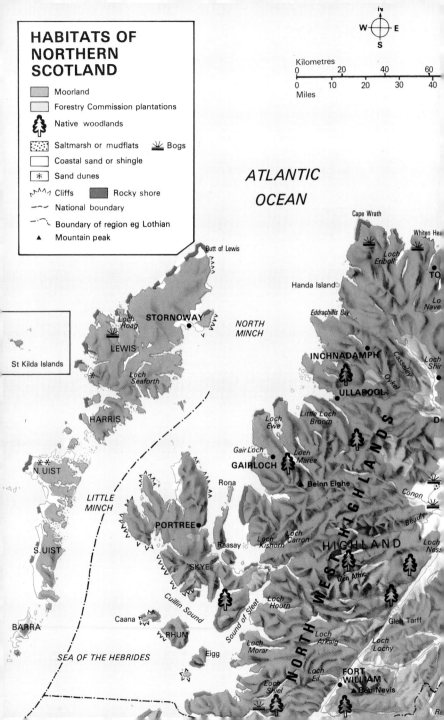

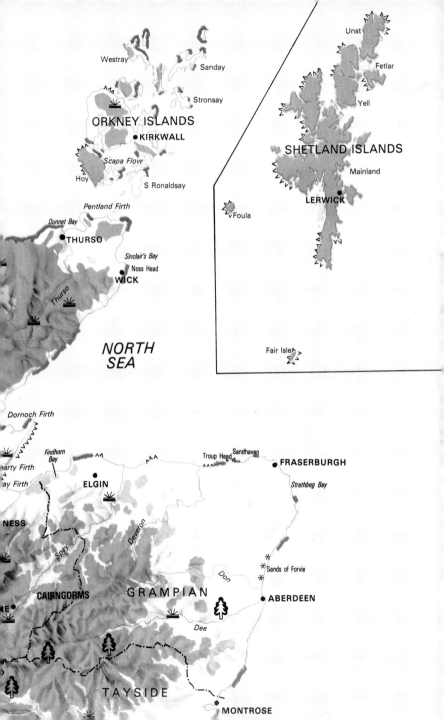

HABITATS OF SOUTHERN SCOTLAND

- Moorland
- Forestry Commission plantations
- Native woodlands
- Saltmarsh or mudflats
- Coastal sand or shingle
- Sand dunes
- Bogs
- Cliffs
- Rocky shore
- National boundary
- Boundary of region eg Lothian
- Mountain peak

Geology and Climate

Geological Features

The rugged mountainous scenery so characteristic of Scotland is due to the presence of old, hard rocks, smoothed by the action of ice during the Ice Ages and worn into sharp crags by the subsequent weathering action of frost and rain.

The further north you travel in Britain, the older the rock formations become. The youngest, softest rocks are found in southern England and the older, hard rocks in northern Scotland – the rocks of the Outer Hebrides being amongst the oldest in the world, over 3000 million years old.

Within Scotland there are three major geological zones: the Highlands, the Central Lowlands and the Southern Uplands. The *Highlands* are predominantly metamorphic rocks; these are rocks which have been subjected to great forces, such as heat and pressure, which have considerably altered their character. The *Central Lowlands* lie on sedimentary rocks; these are rocks which were formed usually as sediments under water, like the gravels and muds being deposited today in lakes, rivers and seas. Sometimes the vegetation of past ages becomes part of this rock formation process: the Coal Measures of the Central Lowlands between Glasgow and Edinburgh were formed in this way. Older sedimentary rocks, which have suffered great pressures causing them to fold, occur in the *Southern Uplands*, where the Galloway Hills, which rise to nearly 900 metres (3000 feet), have many features in common with the Highlands of Scotland.

Throughout Scotland there are rocks known as igneous intrusions. These are rocks which are formed from molten material (magma) originating from deep within the earth. Molten lava may be ejected rapidly as from a volcano, or may solidify well below the surface. The nature of the resultant rock will depend on how quickly it cooled and the minerals it contains. Generally speaking, the "glassy" rocks such as basalt have cooled quickly, whereas the more crystalline rocks such as granite are the result of slow cooling. Metamorphic rocks may have originated as igneous *or* sedimentary rocks before they were altered.

Climate

Another trend across Scotland is the pattern of weather: this time the trend is from west to east. Western Scotland and the Isles are wetter and warmer than the east where the winters are harder with more frosts. It is this colder influence in the east which keeps the Cairngorms covered with snow well into spring.

Altitude also determines climate. The mountain areas generally have more rain in summer, more snow in winter and are several degrees cooler than the valleys or glens at all times of the year. It is often windy on these upland areas and the combination of wind and damp cool air is the main cause of exposure to ill-prepared hill walkers. Conditions may be warm and calm in the glens when one sets out, but the weather at higher altitudes may change quickly (see notes on hill safety on page 122).

Though in general wetter than much of England, the variation in rainfall within Scotland is considerable. In the upland areas of the west coast the annual rainfall is in excess of 3000 mm, whereas on the

Skiing in the Cairngorm mountains in the central Highlands, and boating on Loch Lomond in sunshine in the warmer, wetter west, illustrates the great variation in Scotland's climate and altitude.

coastal plain of the east coast it is little above 600 mm. The Ayrshire coast in south-west Scotland is the exception to the rule, with a warmer and drier summer than most east coast holiday resorts.

The Gulf Stream, or North Atlantic Drift, flows around the shores of Britain eastwards along the Channel and also up the west coast of Scotland, thence into the North Sea. These sea currents help to prevent extremes of temperature off the west coast of Scotland. The winter sea temperatures of the west coast are often in the range of 7° to 9°C – which is the same temperature range recorded off the Channel coasts of England or France.

Air temperatures are also affected by the Gulf Stream: in the winter this results in places such as Lewis in the Western Isles and the Mull of Galloway in south-west Scotland possessing the same average temperatures as London. In the summer the effect is to prevent excessive warming of the sea with resultant lower temperatures than south or east coast areas of Britain. Biologically the effect of these currents has been to carry a number of "southern" marine species northwards to the Scottish shores. Many of these species, susceptible to cold, are able to thrive on the west coast of Scotland; and for some species this is the northernmost limit of their European range.

Throughout Scotland, the months of April, May and June tend on average to be the driest and are ideal for touring holidays. From then on the rainfall increases: by August the average rainfall is double that in May, and October is usually the wettest month of all.

The variations in rock type, of rainfall and degree of frost all combine to influence the wildlife of Scotland. In the south and west of Scotland many plants and animals are found which are more characteristic of the west coast of England, and which are not found elsewhere in Scotland. In contrast, the eastern Highlands possess arctic-alpine plants more reminiscent of Scandinavian flora. This great variety, and Scotland's wild and rugged landscape and scenery, holds a fascination for the visitor during any season of the year.

Mountains and Moorlands

Scotland's mountain ranges are the stronghold of a number of British wildlife species. Although some are very shy, it should be possible to see many of the spectacular upland animals, such as the Red Deer and the Golden Eagle – two animals traditionally associated with the Highland mountains.

Britain has lost many of its larger mammals – Beaver, Wolf, Brown Bear and Elk. Reindeer, thought to have survived here until the twelfth century, have been released on the Cairngorm summits where they now breed successfully.

The feral Goat, thought to have originated from domestic goat stock, now runs wild on the high tops of most upland ranges. Mountain Hares may also be seen on the summit plateaux. The Mountain (or Blue) Hare is specially adapted to life at high altitudes, and its coat turns from brown in summer to white in winter to merge with the snowy landscape. This feature is also characteristic of the Ptarmigan, the game bird of the uplands.

Several species of wader breed on mountains and moorlands, including the Golden Plover, Dunlin and the rare Dotterel. Birds of prey, such as the Golden Eagle, Buzzard, Peregrine Falcon and Hen Harrier, are seen hunting over these areas, and Ravens may still be seen and heard reeling over crags and cliffs, despite their decline in most other areas where open moorland has been given over to commercial forestry.

Moorlands are not as wild and natural as they may appear; indeed, they are carefully managed to provide grazing for sheep and grouse. Before its use for sheep farming, much of the mid-altitude moorland was covered with natural forest or scrub. Traditional management of this moorland involves burning to favour the growth of young nutritious heather. In the drier east, the burning is limited to small blocks of land of just a few hectares. This type of moorland management has been found the most beneficial for grouse – now of considerable economic importance.

▼ Rannoch Moor consists of a complex of moors, bogs, and lochs between the eastern and western Highlands. In some areas peat has eroded, exposing the preserved stumps of ancient Scots Pines.

▲ The magnificent Golden Eagle is most likely to be seen hunting over moors. Its wingspan reaches two metres. It nests on mountain crags.

▲ Female Merlin. The Merlin is Britain's smallest bird of prey (30 cm). It lives on high moorland, but may also be seen on the coast.

▲ Peregrine Falcons nest on the remote rock ledges of sea cliffs and mountains. They hunt over moorland and, in winter, on estuaries.

▲ Hen Harriers are often seen hunting low over moors. In the spring the grey cock performs a spectacular sky-dance courtship display.

▲ Red Grouse: this game bird is found only in the British Isles. It lives on open moorland.

▲ Black Grouse: males (Blackcocks) displaying; their communal display grounds are called leks.

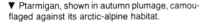

▼ Ptarmigan, shown in autumn plumage, camouflaged against its arctic-alpine habitat.

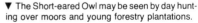

▼ The Short-eared Owl may be seen by day hunting over moors and young forestry plantations.

▲ The Dotterel, a rare, shy wader. It breeds in Britain only in the Scottish Highlands, especially in the Cairngorms, and over-winters in Africa.

▲ The Golden Plover nests on moorlands below 100 metres, whereas the closely-related Dotterel nests on higher moorland and hillsides.

▼ Muirburn is the term given to the burning of heather moorland shown here on the Cairnsmore of Fleet National Nature Reserve, Galloway.

In the wetter west, however, large areas are burnt in an attempt to improve grazing for sheep, though in some cases this appears to be favouring grasses and sedges of little nutrient value, at the expense of heather. The plant life of heavily-burnt areas is often poor, consisting of a few species of moss and lichen growing under the heather in the east, and grasses such as Purple Moor-grass or Matgrass in the west. The invasion of Bracken on the drier slopes of some moorlands has reduced the wildlife interest, since it is poisonous to many plants and animals. The heather moors are at their peak of beauty in August and September, when the flowering heather transforms the whole landscape from green, olive and brown to a blaze of purple and lilac.

The limestone uplands are a great attraction to botanists since a rich variety of plants, some very rare, may be found growing on the ledges and rocky knolls.

Scotland's arctic-alpine flowers have drawn naturalists to the mountain ranges

▲ The Highland Cow is a hardy animal, bred to withstand the biting winds and rain of the exposed moorland. The long horns and coat reveal an ancestry derived from the Ox.

▼ Scottish Black-faced Sheep are found throughout Scotland and are able to live on the poorest moorland pastures. In summer they can be seen wandering on high mountain plateaux.

for centuries. These beautiful flowers, often tiny and growing in masses amongst bare rocks and moss, look too delicate to survive the harsh environment of cliff and ledge. Their survival was threatened by people uprooting whole plants for private collection. Fortunately some of the finest displays are now protected, for example on Ben Lawers, where visitors may still enjoy the beautiful alpine plants blooming on the mountain ledges.

Although Scotland's wild mountainous and moorland areas still support some of Britain's most spectacular animals and plants, they are by no means safe. Birds of prey are still persecuted on some estates and have lost large tracts of their open habitat to forestry plantations. Even on the high plateaux, the development of skiing and tourist facilities are considered by many to be potential threats to the flora and fauna. Yet, with careful planning, it should be possible for people to enjoy the spectacle of upland wildlife without endangering its longterm survival.

▲ The Adder, often seen sunning itself on rocky knolls. Britain's only poisonous snake, it generally moves away when disturbed.

▲ The Mountain Hare (or Blue Hare), seen in its winter coat. Brown during the summer, it has shorter ears and legs than the Brown Hare.

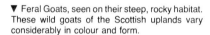

▼ Feral Goats, seen on their steep, rocky habitat. These wild goats of the Scottish uplands vary considerably in colour and form.

▲ Red Deer hinds: the strongest stags gather a harem of hinds in the autumn which they defend against other stags during the rut by roaring, grunting and ritualized fights.

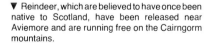

▼ Reindeer, which are believed to have once been native to Scotland, have been released near Aviemore and are running free on the Cairngorm mountains.

▲ Yellow Saxifrage grows on rocks near springs and in damp flushes where drainage from richer rocks brings nutrients to the surface.

▲ Dwarf Cornel often grows half-hidden under Heather or Bilberry on poor acid soils. In autumn the leaves turn bright red.

▲ Tufted Saxifrage is a rare arctic-alpine plant which grows on sheltered mountain ledges in the Cairngorms and Ben Nevis ranges.

▲ Moss Campion: cushions of these bright pink flowers may be seen in summer growing in masses on mountain crags and on sea cliffs.

▲ Mountain Avens, a plant that grows on lime-rich rocks and flowers in early summer.

▲ Cloudberry grows on upland moors; its red fruit turns golden-yellow when ripe.

▼ Mountain Everlasting, also called Catsear or Catsfoot, is a common plant of mountain slopes.

▼ Purple Oxytropis is found on limestone outcrops in mountains and on coastal headlands.

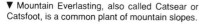

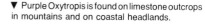

Lochs and Rivers

Scotland's clear pure water plays an important economic role. The mighty salmon which thrive in the clean, fast-flowing rivers are now a world-wide tourist attraction, and the many whisky distilleries, for which Scotland is also internationally renowned, each use water from a different Scottish glen to ensure their distinctive flavours.

The golden or brown colour of many Scottish lochs and rivers is due to staining which results from water passing through peaty soils, especially peat bogs. In these mainly upland lochs and rivers the water is acid and contains few nutrients, but nonetheless supports a variety of interesting wildlife. An even greater diversity is found in the richer lowland waters or those which flow from lime-rich rocks.

In many areas of Scotland, Otters may still be observed along rivers, though the Mink is more commonly seen; Mink are not native animals of Scotland, but having escaped from mink farms, have rapidly colonized the mainland. Deer often visit

▲ The Osprey now breeds in several parts of Scotland; it hunts over lochs and estuaries.

▼ A view of Beinn Eighe from Loch Clair in the north-west Highlands. Beinn Eighe is botanically rich with arctic-alpine flora, Scots Pine and Birch woodland.

lochs and may sometimes be seen swimming across the larger lochs and rivers.

The waterways of Scotland are the haunts of many birds. The handsome Dipper is often seen by rapid tumbling streams and rivers, flittering from one boulder to another or bouncing its body up and down before walking into the river. Herons fish the rivers and lochs and Cormorants often visit lochs well inland.

One of the great attractions for bird watchers in Scotland is the Osprey which breeds regularly here, and which can be observed at Loch Garten (under the protection of the Royal Society for the Protection of Birds). During the winter many lochs are the home for thousands of wildfowl from the arctic regions. The common ducks of Scottish lochs are Mallard, Teal, Goldeneye, Tufted Duck and Wigeon.

Very few wild geese breed in Britain, but several species over-winter regularly in Scotland: Pink-footed and Greylag Geese are found in several localities and Greenland White-fronted Geese occur in Kirkcudbrightshire. Wetland habitats often attract flocks of Whooper Swans, while Little and Great Crested Grebes, Moorhens and Coots commonly breed by lochs and streams. The rare Slavonian Grebe can occasionally be spotted on northern waters, and both Black-throated and Red-throated Divers are found on lochs in the north-west of Scotland. Several species of

wader breed at the edge of lochs, where the sight of Common Sandpipers displaying, or the sound of piping Oystercatchers, is commonplace.

Salmon and Trout are found in all the major river systems and many other species of freshwater fish have been introduced or have colonized Scottish waters. The waters are also interesting for their insect life, such as Water Beetles and the nymphal stages of Stonefly, Mayfly and Caddisfly, and the Damselfly is often seen near the water.

The plant life in Scottish rivers is often sparse, but the banksides are amongst the richest botanical hunting grounds. Remnants of ancient woodlands clothe the higher reaches, whilst the herb-rich banks and meadows of the lower reaches are stippled with colour during the summer months. Marsh Marigold, Globeflower, Meadowsweet and Yellow Flag may intermingle with introduced species such as Himalayan Balsam, Lupin and Monkey Flower to give a tapestry of colour. Further upstream, shingle banks, otherwise green with moss, grass or sedge, may be colonized by a colourful alpine such as Yellow Mountain Saxifrage. The vegetation surrounding lochs where the water is acid and where the substrate is rocky may be very poorly developed. In contrast, the lowland lochs may be very rich and surrounded by large reed beds.

▼ In Scotland the Heron (*left*) may be seen fishing in many kinds of watery habitats from tiny moorland burns to expansive estuaries. It usually nests in colonies in trees. The Kingfisher (*centre*) prefers slow-running rivers, lochs and gravel pits. Vulnerable to hard winters, it tends to be confined to the milder lowlands of the south and west. (*Left*) Reed bed on the edge of a loch: Reed Buntings, Sedge Warblers, even the rare Spotted Crake may live here.

▲ Black-throated (*left*) and Red-throated (*right*) Divers may be seen on highland lochs during the summer when they nest near the shore. The Highlands are their only British breeding territory, and they winter at sea. Well-adapted to swimming and diving, they rarely visit land except to breed.

▲ Great Crested Grebes nest on shallow lochs amongst reeds and rushes; they are found throughout southern Scotland.

▲ The Whooper Swan is a winter visitor to several Scottish lochs. This magnificent bird has occasionally stopped to breed in Scotland.

▲Female Goosander:its British breeding range is confined to Scotland; it nests in tree holes.

▲ Wigeon drake. Wigeon breed by lochs; in winter large flocks are found on lochs and estuaries.

▼ The Grey Wagtail is usually seen near water, and breeds by fast-flowing streams.

▼ The Dipper can be seen bobbing up and down on rocks in the middle of fast-flowing streams.

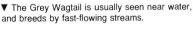

▲ Otters are found along rivers and on the coast especially in the north and west of Scotland. They are shy and generally nocturnal.

▲ Fishing for Salmon and Trout in Scottish rivers. Scotland's superb fishing attracts tourists from many countries.

▲ Mink are now found in every district of the Scottish mainland. Difficult to control, they are considered a threat to native wildlife.

▲ Damselflies may be seen hovering and darting along the shores of lochs and by rivers, catching insects in mid-air.

▼ The Globeflower (*left*) grows in damp pastures and by upland lochs. The dainty Water Lobelia (*centre*), an aquatic plant, may be seen in acid lochs in western Scotland. This Monkey Flower (*right*) is one of three species (originally introduced as garden flowers) found growing in wet places in Scotland.

The Coast

Scotland's long, varied and relatively unspoilt coast offers an ideal habitat for wildlife. The wide range of marine life is partly due to the Gulf Stream, which provides the warmer conditions necessary for the survival of species more typical of southern waters (this is especially true of western Scotland). It is also due to the lack of pollution along most of the coast.

Rocky shores dominate the western and northern coast; here, intertidal rock pools are fascinating havens for marine life. On the shore too, different plants and animals are found in different zones between the high and low water marks. Specialist field guides (see page 122) explain the zonation and show where the different seaweeds, barnacles, and molluscs live in relation to high or low tide marks. The strand line is another attraction, where fish egg cases, cuttlefish and even stranded jellyfish are washed up amongst the seaweed.

Off the west coast there is a good chance of seeing a Killer Whale, a Porpoise or a school of White-beaked Dolphins performing spectacular leaps. Both Common and Grey Seals may be observed around the coast and breeding colonies are found on the mainland, the Western Isles, Orkneys and Shetlands. Common Seals tend to favour the sheltered waters of estuaries, sea lochs and sand banks whereas the Grey Seal is more typical of exposed rocky coasts.

The long stretches of cliff-lined shore and craggy offshore islands are famous for their mixed colonies of thousands of sea birds. Amongst the species that may nest near one another are Guillemots, Razorbills, Puffins, Fulmars, Kittiwakes, Herring Gulls, Great Black-backed Gulls and Shags. Some of the world's largest Gannet colonies are found in Scotland's rocky islands and stacks. The largest colony is found on the St Kilda Islands, where over 40,000 pairs of Gannets and the same number in total of Guillemots, Razorbills, Puffins and Kittiwakes may nest near one another.

Other cliff-nesting birds include the rare Chough, the red-billed and red-legged member of the crow family, and Ravens, now very rare, may nest here, especially on the west and north coasts. Hooded Crow, Jackdaw, and, more rarely, Peregrine Falcon, Buzzard and Golden Eagle,

▼ Cliffs of the Shetland coast, where large sea bird colonies are found. In the moorland behind, Snowy Owl, Great Skua and Whimbrel breed.

▼ Grey Seals can be seen along many rocky coasts. The Grey has a straight head profile which distinguishes it from the Common Seal.

▼ The Gannet, the largest British sea bird, has a wingspan of nearly two metres.

may nest on cliff sites. An attempt is being made to reintroduce the White-tailed Sea Eagle to the Western Isles.

Cliffs are often very rich in flowers, especially those on neutral or lime-rich rocks. Bird colonies may also enrich cliff sites, the guano being a rich source of nutrients; seeds carried in the birds' guano are probably responsible for introducing several untypical species of plants to mainland cliff sites and offshore islands. Some species that grow on Scottish cliff tops are more typical of other habitats: alpines, well adapted to harsh, exposed environments, may grow here, including Starry Saxifrage, Moss Campion, Mountain Avens and Mountain Sorrel. In contrast, woodland plants like Primrose, Red Campion and Wood Vetch grow on sheltered cliffs. More typical of their cliff habitat are Stonecrops, Thrift, Roseroot, Lovage and Spring Squill. The tiny Scottish Primrose with its minute purple-red flower is often lost even in the short turf of a cliff ledge. When exploring cliffs, keep on well-marked paths away from the edge.

▲ Puffins retain their bright-striped bill only during the breeding season. They nest in large colonies in burrows on grassy cliffs and grass-covered rocky islands. Puffins winter at sea.

▲ The Fulmar nests on cliffs and winters at sea. Its breeding range is spreading southwards.

▼ Gannet colonies like this one on Bass Rock may contain several thousand pairs of birds.

▲ Black Guillemot: breeds north and west coasts.

▲ Razorbills often breed with other sea birds.

▼ Kittiwakes (*left*) breed in large colonies on cliffs, often on narrow ledges. The Shag (*centre*) is found on rocky coasts. The Scottish Primrose (*right*) grows on cliff tops on the north coast.

▼ From April to August, sea cliffs can be rich with colour as coastal and mountain plants grow in this harsh habitat without competition from taller but less hardy species.

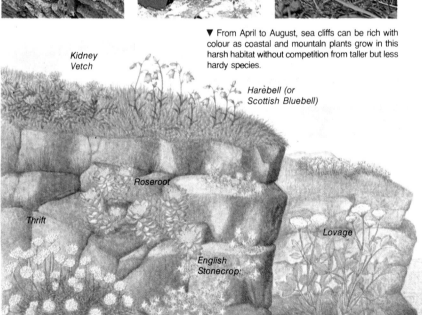

Kidney Vetch

Harebell (or Scottish Bluebell)

Roseroot

Thrift

Lovage

English Stonecrop

▲ Male Common Scoter: Scoters breed around lakes, but are essentially sea ducks – up to 10,000 may reside in the Murray Firth in January.

▲ Male Red-breasted Merganser; the smaller female has a brown crest. It is seen on the sea, on estuaries and occasionally on inland rivers.

▲ The Oyster Plant grows in mats on shingle beaches; its flowers are pinkish when first open.

▼ Eider Ducks often breed in dunes. Thousands over-winter in the Tay estuary mussel beds.

In between the headlands are numerous bays with beaches of shingle or sand, both with a very specialized flora. On sand, plants like Sea Rocket, Prickly Saltwort and species of Scurvy-grass may survive the drought, lack of nutrients and shifting sand substrate. Shingle is more stable and supports a wider range of plants including Sea Campion, Silverweed, Scentless Mayweed and the Scottish speciality, the Oyster Plant.

Long stretches of sandy coastline backed by well-formed sand dunes are also found in Scotland. These are rich wildlife habitats and several are protected as nature reserves. Nearest to the sea grow the dune-forming Marram Grass and Sand Couchgrass, which stabilize the sand. Next grow the dune species including Spear Thistle, Sea Storksbill and Sea Plantain. Meadow species are found further inland on drier dune pasture and a number of orchids may grow here, including Early Purple, Common Spotted, Fragrant and Frog Orchids.

Dune systems contain a variety of habitats. Lime-rich areas may exist where shell-sand deposits have formed, giving

▲ The rare and protected Natterjack Toad, found in saltmarsh and sand dunes in the south-west.

▼ Arctic Terns nest on beaches and rocky shores and will boldly defend their territories.

rise to the interesting plant communities of dune pasture. Other areas, however, are acid and nutrient-poor and on older stable dunes may develop into heathland. Wet hollows (called dune slacks) are important for a wide range of marsh and bog plants. Within dune systems, maritime scrub may also form, with the growth of shrubs like Sea Buckthorn, Burnet Rose and Hawthorn, and trees such as Birch, Alder and Willow.

The sand dunes are also important as nesting places for a few birds, the most famous being the Eider Duck. The Sands of Forvie in the Grampian region possess the largest mainland breeding colony in Britain. All the British species of terns may be seen in Scotland on sand or shingle beaches. The handsome Shelduck usually nests in a rabbit burrow amongst sand dunes. Black-headed Gull colonies are also found in dune areas.

Scotland has two other interesting coastal habitats – sea lochs and also machair. The sea lochs are miniature fjords, extremely sheltered in comparison with the coast, with a great diversity of marine life. In winter, sea lochs provide shelter for many thousands of duck, easily viewed from vantage points on the shores.

Machair is an unusual habitat of soil derived from shell-sand and makes up the coastal fringe of several islands in the Western Isles – like Uist, Tiree and Barra. Machair may be up to one kilometre wide and is usually part of the crofting land. Its lime-rich soil supports many plants, giving colour to an otherwise bleak landscape.

▲ Sand dunes with Marram Grass, of great importance in stabilizing blown sand and forming dunes. Dunes are interesting botanical hunting grounds; May to August is the richest time.

▲ Burnet Rose: this dainty rose species forms small bushes (20–50 cm high) in exposed dry places like sand dunes and rocky coasts, and may also be found inland.

▼ The Common Spotted Orchid grows in many lime-rich habitats and is found in dune systems, as is the Fragrant Orchid (not shown).

▼ The Northern Marsh Orchid is often found in damp dune slacks and on machair where shell sand deposits produce a rich, fertile habitat.

Estuaries and Saltmarsh

Scottish estuaries, known in Scotland as firths, are famous for their over-wintering wildfowl and wader population. The great tidal range of some estuaries (up to ten metres in the Solway Firth) exposes vast mud and sand banks, which offer safe roosting and feeding for many thousands of birds. The Scottish estuaries maintain a significant proportion of the European population of several wildfowl and wader species, so Britain has an international responsibility to safeguard them. These important estuaries include the Solway Firth and the Inner Clyde on the west coast and the Firth of Forth, Moray Firth, Cromarty Firth, Firth of Tay and the Montrose Basin on the east coast. Each attracts many thousands of wildfowl and waders, peak numbers for the Solway Firth reaching 150,000.

The food to support the enormous numbers of birds is found in the mud of the estuaries. Estuarine mudflats are one of the most food-rich habitats in the world – six times more productive than an average wheat field and twenty times more than the open sea. The richness is a result of constant supply of nutrients from both the sea and the rivers flowing into the estuary.

These vast bare expanses of mud are swarming with the small animals which are the diet of birds. Tens or even hundreds of thousands of minute invertebrates may live in one cubic metre.

The length of a wader's bill is related to its food. Short-billed birds like the Plovers feed on sea snails and other animals found close to the surface of the mud, whereas Dunlin, Redshank and other medium-billed birds probe deeper down to obtain crustacea, small worms and molluscs. Long-billed waders such as Curlew and Godwits probe deeper, often in pools or on the tide edge, seeking large marine worms.

Several ducks, such as Shelduck, Pintail, Teal and Mallard may all depend on mud-dwelling organisms at certain times of the year. Likewise fish, eels and shrimps attract diving birds. Mergansers find rich feeding in the shallow creeks, and Terns are often seen diving from flight to catch

▼ A sheltered estuary bay. In large estuaries, these offer safe winter refuge for hundreds of waders.

small fish. Herons also visit estuaries, and Kingfishers may winter here. Ospreys fish estuaries during their spring and autumn migrations (they winter in Africa). Two species of over-wintering swans – Whooper and Bewick's – find estuaries a safe roosting place, especially when inland lochs suffer disturbance.

Extensive saltmarsh (known as merse in the South) occurs in the shallow sheltered waters of estuaries and at the head of lochs. These saltmarshes are often dominated by just a few plant species: Glasswort is one of the primary colonizers, followed by a sward of Sea Poa Grass. Beyond this fringe the merse is richer, with Scurvy-grass, Sea Aster, Seablite, Sea Plantain, Sea Arrow-grass and Thrift, which eventually merge with meadow species or, in some cases, sedges, rushes or reeds.

The saltmarsh vegetation is important for duck such as Wigeon and Pintail as well as for geese such as Pink-footed, Greylag and Barnacle Geese. Although geese may feed on saltmarshes, the prime use is as a safe roost, with the main feeding areas often several miles inland. Movement from the roost to the feeding ground is at dawn and the return at sunset.

These estuaries and saltmarshes, which provide a vital habitat for many species of wildlife, are continually threatened by human activities. Reclamation for agricultural land, industrial development, pollution, tourism and recreation may all harm the wildlife interests of estuaries. Although their future is far from secure, government and voluntary conservation bodies are continually striving to safeguard the most valuable examples of these estuarine habitats.

▲ Dunlin flocks flashing grey and white as they turn and wheel. Dunlin over-winter in large flocks along coasts and estuaries.

▲ The Ringed Plover nests on shingle or sand. It may be seen paddling wet sand or mud with one foot to bring its prey to the surface.

▲ Knot and Oystercatchers: mixed flocks of waders are regularly seen in autumn and winter.

▼ Oystercatchers in a typical high tide roost site. They form large flocks in winter.

▼ The Oystercatcher, which in Scotland breeds inland (rivers, lochs, moors) and on the coast.

▲ The Barnacle Goose is a winter visitor to Scotland, occurring in large flocks especially on the west and south-west coasts.

▲ The Greylag Goose, Britain's only indigenous goose, breeds mainly in Scotland on moorland near to lochs.

▼ Saltmarshes form on estuaries and at the head of sea lochs. Characteristic of these marshes is a dense sward of Sea Poa and Creeping Fescue Grasses, which may cover extensive areas of mudflats.

▲ Barnacle Geese feeding on saltmarsh grasses. Barnacle Geese stay in Scotland (mainly the west and south-west) until well after Easter before flying to their arctic breeding grounds.

▲ The Pink-footed Goose, a winter visitor to Scotland from the arctic tundra. It feeds on stubble fields during the day and roosts on coastal mudflats at night.

▼ Caerlaverock National Nature Reserve consists of a maze of intertidal sandbanks, channels and saltmarsh, very attractive to wildfowl and waders in the winter.

Forests

Although much of lowland Scotland was once covered by deciduous woodland, most people associate Scotland with coniferous forests. Today there are few examples of true native pine forests in Scotland, and most of the large areas of forest are plantations of non-native trees such as spruce and larch. These artificial forests are not as rich in birdlife as native woodland and their dense planting quickly suppresses any plant life. Nevertheless, plantation edges and rides are valuable habitats and have helped several species of birds including Sparrowhawk and Hen Harrier as well as those typically Scottish mammals, the Wild Cat and Pine Marten, by providing safe, undisturbed habitats where they can breed. Roe Deer and Red Deer have taken full advantage of the cover afforded by the new plantations. Both these species of deer have to be controlled. Other deer that may be encountered in a few Scottish woodlands are Fallow and Sika Deer.

▼ A spider's web strung between branches is outlined by the early morning dew.

Orb-web spiders are particularly common in woodlands since this habitat provides them with suitable structures onto which they can fix their webs, as well as harbouring an abundance of insect prey.

▲ A Sitka Spruce plantation in Galloway: Scotland's new forests consist of large plantations of fast-growing, introduced conifers.

▲ Mixed deciduous woodland such as this one, in which Oak dominates, once covered vast areas of lowland Scotland but are now rare.

▲ Loch Lomond: a famous beauty spot, yet few people are aware of the great variety of habitats and wildlife to be found along its shore.

▼ A young Roe Deer: the white-spotted coat lasts three months and serves as camouflage in the sun-dappled clearings of the forest.

The true native Caledonian pine forests of Scotland remain only as relics of much larger forests. Today, the Scots Pine woodlands of the Spey and Dee Valleys, the slopes of Beinn Eighe and Glen Affric are amongst the best examples. These are open woods with prolific moss and heather growth covering the ground. Several rare plants are found in ancient pine woods, such as various species of Wintergreen, Twinflower and the orchids – Lesser Twayblade, Creeping Lady's Tresses and Coral-root. Most of the birds of natural conifer forests adapt quickly to the new plantations, but the Scottish Crossbill and the Crested Tit are still largely confined to the old Caledonian forests in Scotland.

The Capercaillie, whose British range is confined to Scotland, may be seen in the shelter of Scots Pine forests. Other game birds are Black Grouse, Woodcock and Pheasant, usually seen at the edges of forests and in young plantations.

▲ Wild Cats thrive in the cover of forestry plantations; they also hunt in open moorland.

▲ Pine Martens prefer mixed woodland, hunting birds and rodents in trees and on the ground.

▲ Male Capercaillie: a game bird of coniferous forests, it feeds on young shoots and berries.

▼ The Red Squirrel (*left*) lives in coniferous forests. The Great Spotted Woodpecker (*centre*) is found throughout Scotland. The Crested Tit (*right*) is confined to pine forests of northern Scotland.

▲ Female Sparrowhawk: this woodland bird of prey often finds nest sites at the edges of conifer plantations.

▲ The Buzzard, seen mainly in areas where moorland, mountain crags and forested areas are found in close proximity.

▲ The Long-eared Owl favours conifer forests, and nests in the old nests of other birds. It hunts (usually at night) for small rodents.

▲ The Woodcock nests on the ground. These secretive woodland birds are more often seen in spring when the male performs his display flight.

▲ Male Redstart. This bird, a summer migrant to Scotland, favours old deciduous woodland.

▲ Nesting female Siskin. Siskins are resident all year in Scotland.

▼ Scottish Crossbills: female is shown on the left of male. Crossbills nest in conifers.

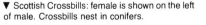

▼ The Goldcrest is one bird that has benefited from large-scale coniferous afforestation.

In the few remaining oak woodlands there is to be found some of the richest plant and animal life in Scotland. Many of the typically British woodland flowers are well represented in Scotland, including Dog's Mercury and Bluebell (called Wild Hyacinth in Scotland). Other woodland flowers include Wood Anemone, Wood Sorrel and Wood Stitchwort, all having distinctive white flowers; Wood Garlic, whose large white flowers have a characteristic garlic smell, and Wood Speedwell with its dainty lilac flower. The dampness of many western deciduous woodlands has provided a suitable habitat for the luxuriant

▲ Wood Anemones are typical flowers of deciduous woods, flowering from April to May.

▲ Primroses are found in woods and hedgerows, and along the coasts in western Scotland.

▼ Wood Cranesbill grows in damp woods and in more open habitats on sea cliffs and mountains.

growth of many lichen species on the trees. Similarly a wide variety of mosses and liverworts grow around their roots.

Scrub woodlands of Birch and Alder may also have a rich flora especially on moist ground. Here Marsh Thistle, Marsh Hawksbeard and Golden Saxifrage grow amongst grasses and sedges.

Oak is rarely present on its own and is often in mixed woodlands accompanied by Birch, Ash, Aspen and Wych Elm with Alder and Willow on wetter ground. Rowan and Holly are often present as a shrub layer. These deciduous woodlands are extremely rich in insect life and as a consequence the numbers of spiders and birds which feed on insects are also high.

Red Squirrels are typical of coniferous and mixed woodland and appear to be holding their own against the Grey Squirrel which has replaced them in much of Britain. Fox, Hare, Weasel, Rabbit, Stoat and Badger may be seen in woods.

Natural woodland in Scotland is still disappearing at an alarming rate and much effort will be needed to secure its future against the demands of commercial forestry and agricultural development.

▲ Bracken is common in open woodland with light, dry soil; it is intolerant of dense forest shade.

▼ The Scotch Argus butterfly is most abundant on hilly wooded ground in the west of Scotland.

Bogs

The soggy ground and bleak landscape of the Scottish bogs make them an unpopular place to explore, the difficult walking terrain preventing most people from venturing far off the main roads and tracks. Yet to others the bogs hold a fascination, their remoteness and solitude representing a very special part of the Scottish landscape. With care, one can explore boggy areas away from the tracks by using rocks and hummocks as stepping stones. A greater range of the flora and fauna special to the bogs can then be seen.

Bogs form in areas where hard rocks and high rainfall provide a constant wetness in the soils. A combination of wetness and acidity actually prevents plants from decomposing. The remnants of dead plants remain each year. The plant growth of any one year will develop on top of the undecayed remains of previous years in such a way that peat contains within itself its own vegetational history. This makes undisturbed peat particularly valuable to the scientist. Studies of peat borings have provided much of the evidence of vegetational change in Scotland, in some cases as far back as the last Ice Age.

The wet acid conditions of peat bogs provide few mineral nutrients for plants, and a specific range of plants adapted to the conditions has evolved. Sundew and Butterwort are good examples: both are insectivorous plants which compensate for the poor nutrient levels in peat bogs by catching and digesting insects. Other

▼ Amongst the wildlife adapted to and dependent on bogs are insectivorous plants (like Butterwort and Bladderwort), bog mosses, and certain species of insects and spiders. Wading birds find safe refuge here for breeding and deer may find food and shelter in harsh weather.

Red Deer

Meadow Pipit

Greenshank

Bladderwort

Cotton Grass

Large Heath Butterfly

Bog Asphodel

Pale Butterwort

Cross-leaved Heath

Sphagnum Moss

plants common on bogs are heathers, sedges and mosses. The bog mosses are particularly abundant and the different species are adapted to different degrees of waterlogging.

Many insects and spiders live amongst these bog plants; some, like the rare Blue Aeshna Dragonfly, are restricted to this habitat alone. Red Deer often graze on bogs, especially during the winter. Several wading birds, including Curlew, Golden Plover and Greenshank, find safe nesting sites on peatlands.

Peat bogs still cover large areas of Scotland but modern land use is rapidly destroying this important habitat. Drainage, fertilization and afforestation all alter the very special conditions needed for peat formation. In order to protect representative examples of peat bogs several areas in Scotland have been declared nature reserves.

▲ Peat is commercially extracted for horticultural use. In small isolated communities however it is still also cut for its traditional use as domestic fuel for heating and cooking. This picture, taken in the Shetland Isles, shows peat piled on the roadside to dry out.

▲ The Common Frog lives in any moist habitat including bogs; it breeds in pools ranging from coastal marshes to small mountain "lochans".

▲ The Heath Spotted Orchid grows on acid soils including bogs. Widespread in Scotland, it grows in peaty soils up to 1000 metres (3000 feet).

▼ Oblong-leaved Sundew (*left*): sundews are insectivorous plants, trapping insects on sticky glistening hairs on the leaves. Bogbean (*centre*) is commonly found in bog pools even at high altitudes. Cotton Grass (*right*) seen with its feathery seedheads is sometimes abundant on bogs.

Common Species of the Countryside and Seashore

Some of Britain's animals and plants can be found only in certain regions, or are more easily found in some areas than in others. Living alongside these rare or local species are, of course, many animals and plants which are fairly widespread throughout the country. The more common species of British birds, wild flowers, trees, butterflies, mammals and seashore animals are illustrated on the following pages. These illustrations form a basic field guide to the majority of the regions in Britain.

The captions to the bird illustrations indicate the bird's usual haunts, and if it is seen only in certain seasons, this fact is mentioned. Measurements indicate the size of the bird from the tip of the beak to the end of the tail. Notes to aid identification of the species are also included.

The mammals that are illustrated are accompanied by captions which indicate their average size. Those for hoofed mammals indicate their height at the shoulder. Others indicate the length of their bodies from nose to rump. The captions also give an indication as to when the animal is most active and therefore most easily observed.

The wild flowers are grouped according to their commonest colours; their most frequently used names are given in the captions, along with their habitats, the months in which they flower and their height or the length of creeping stems if they grow horizontally.

The illustrations of butterflies frequently show them on the plants they prefer to visit. The captions indicate the butterflies' usual habitats, the months when they are most frequently seen, and their wingspan.

Information about the sizes of the seashore animals are detailed in their captions, while the height of the trees is given on page 96. Selected identifying characteristics are given in the captions to the trees.

A hedgerow in early summer—one of the countryside's most rewarding habitats, since it shelters a wide variety of species. This illustration features some of the common, widespread plants and animals included in the following pages.

Birds

Canada Goose ▶
Fields and marshes near water; parks. Brown wings and body. Introduced from Canada. 95 cm.

Shag ▶
Rocky coats, where it nests in colonies. Has crest only in breeding season. Flies low, close to the water. 78 cm.

Cormorant ▶
Near the sea and some large inland waters. Has white thigh patch in breeding season. Larger than Shag. 92 cm.

Spring

◀ Mute Swan
Wide rivers, lakes, town parks. Not, as its name implies, mute. Britain's most common swan. 152 cm.

Mallard ▲
Inland waters and estuaries.
Purplish-blue wing patch seen in
flight. 58 cm.

▼ Wigeon
Near sea, especially in winter; lakes and
marshes. Seen August-April; a few stay
to breed. 46 cm.

◄ Pintail
Lakes and marshes, near coast in winter.
Pointed tail and long, elegant neck. Seen
September-March; a few stay to breed.
66 cm.

Shoveler ►
Quiet lakes and shallow water. Large,
heavy bill. Pale blue forewings of both
male and female show in flight. 51 cm.

▼ Teal
Inland waters and estuaries. The
smallest duck in Britain. Dark bill.
Quick and agile in flight. 35 cm.

▲ Tufted Duck
Lakes, ponds, gravel pits and parks.
Dumpy, active diving duck. Note female's
yellow eye. 43 cm.

▼ Pochard
Lakes and backwaters. In flight, both sexes have dark wings with paler grey central bar. 46 cm.

♂

♀

♂

▲ Shelduck
Coasts and estuaries, often in flocks; also large inland lakes. Female has no red knob on bill. 61 cm.

♀

♂

▲ Red-breasted Merganser
Coastal areas; wooded lakes, rivers, in breeding season. 58 cm.

Grey Heron ▶
Near water: rivers, lakes and seashores. Head is drawn back in flight. 92 cm.

Summer

Winter

▼ Little Grebe
Inland waters. Secretive and hard to spot. 27 cm.

▲ Great Crested Grebe
Inland waters, sometimes on sea in winter. 48 cm.

Winter

Summer

Buzzard ▼
Often seen soaring over moors
and farmland. Rare in east and
south-east England. 54 cm.

▼ Kestrel
Moors, coasts, farmland;
some nest in towns.
Hovers when hunting.
34 cm.

Coot ▶
Lakes, reservoirs,
open water.
Larger, heavier
bird than
Moorhen.
38 cm.

▲ Moorhen
Ponds, lakes and streams. 33 cm.

◀ Partridge
Farmland, moors. Small head,
short tail and legs. Often in
small groups. 30 cm.

♂

▼ Pheasant
Farmland, scrub,
woodland. Males can
have white neckring.
Male 87 cm, female
58 cm.

♀

Summer

Winter

◀ **Redshank**
Seashores and wet
meadows. Probes in
mud. 28 cm.

▼ **Oystercatcher**
Seashores, estuaries. Often
in groups. White band on
throat in winter. 43 cm.

▲ **Turnstone**
Shingle or rocky coasts. Turns over stones,
seaweed, to find food. 23 cm.

Common Sandpiper ▲
Rivers, streams and lakes.
Seen April-October; a few in
winter. 20 cm.

▼ **Ringed Plover**
Sandy and muddy shores.
In summer, white wing bar
shows in flight. 19 cm.

*Adult in
summer*

Juvenile

Lapwing ▲
Farmland, marshes, mudflats. 30 cm.

Curlew ▶
Mudflats and estuaries in winter; farmland,
moors in breeding season. Rare in East
Anglia and the South-East as a breeder.
Britain's largest wader. 48-64 cm.

Winter

**▲ Bar-tailed
Godwit**
Coastal mudflats and
estuaries. Smaller
than Black-tailed
Godwit. 37 cm.

Black-tailed Godwit ▶
Coasts in winter; inland lakes, marshes in
breeding season. White wing bar in
summer. 41 cm.

Winter

◀ Whimbrel
Coastal mudflats
and estuaries;
meadows near the
sea. 40 cm.

Woodcock ▼
Damp woods; not
seen on shore.
Secretive.
34 cm.

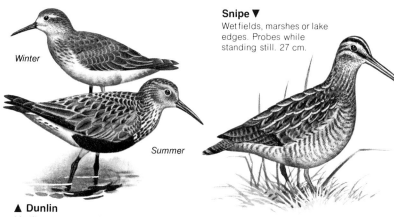

Snipe ▼
Wet fields, marshes or lake edges. Probes while standing still. 27 cm.

▲ Dunlin
Mudflats and estuaries. Common winter shorebird; less common in summer. 19 cm.

Winter

Greenshank ▼
Coasts, marshes. Seen chiefly on migration. Some breed in Scotland. 30 cm.

▲ Sanderling
Sandy shores along coasts. Seen August-May. Short, straight beak. 20 cm.

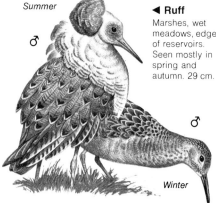

Summer

♂

◄ Ruff
Marshes, wet meadows, edges of reservoirs. Seen mostly in spring and autumn. 29 cm.

♂

Winter

▼ Knot
Sand or mudflats in estuaries. Larger than Dunlin. Seen mostly August-May. 25 cm.

Winter

▼ Common Tern
Near sea; also nests inland in Scotland.
Seen April-October. 34 cm.

Summer

◀ Little Tern
Shingle beaches. Never
has full black cap like other
terns. Seen
April-September. 24 cm.

Summer

Herring Gull ▼
Coastal ports and seaside
towns. Wingtips are black
with white spots. 56 cm.

◀ Black-headed Gull
Inland and near the sea. Dark
brown "hood" in summer
only. 37 cm.

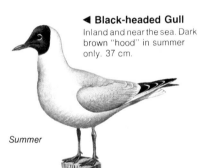

Summer

Summer

Common Gull ▶
Coasts; often inland in
winter. Smaller and
less widespread than
Herring Gull. 41 cm.

Lesser
Black-backed
Gull ▶
Coasts and inland.
Mainly a summer
visitor. 53 cm.

▼ Guillemot
Rocky coasts. Neck and
throat are white in winter.
Seen at cliff sites
December-August. 42 cm.

◄ Fulmar
Rocky coasts. Nests on cliffs.
Always sits, never stands.
Mostly out at sea in winter.
47 cm.

Puffin ►
Rocky islands and
sea cliffs. Colourful
bill in summer.
30 cm.

Summer

Summer

▼ Collared Dove
Large gardens, parks and
farmland. Long white tail with
black base. 30 cm.

◄ Stock Dove
Woods and cliffs;
sometimes in towns.
Darker, smaller bird than
Woodpigeon. 33 cm.

Rock Dove ▼
Coasts, usually on sea
cliffs. Town pigeons are
descended from these
birds. 33 cm.

Woodpigeon ►
Farmland, woods and
towns. White neck
patch on adult. 41 cm.

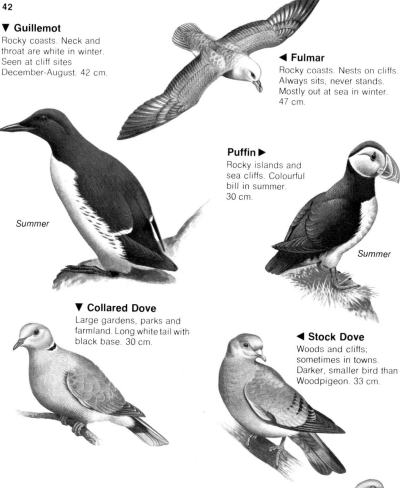

▼ Short-eared Owl
Open country. Hunts in
day-time or at dusk. 37 cm.

◄ Barn Owl
Open country,
especially
farmland. Mostly
nocturnal. 34 cm.

**◄ Long-eared
Owl**
Edges of woods.
Underside all dark.
Nocturnal. 34 cm.

Little Owl ▼
Farmland and wooded
country. Underside is
streaked. Often seen in
daylight. 22 cm.

▲ Tawny Owl
Parks, woodland and
farmland; sometimes towns.
Large head. Nocturnal. 38 cm

◄ Kingfisher
Near rivers and
lakes; seashore in
winter. Dives from
low perch or from a
hover. 17 cm.

▼ Cuckoo
Anywhere in countryside.
Male's song is well known.
April-September. 30 cm.

44

Swift ▶
Breeds mainly in towns;
may fly over countryside.
Seen end of April-
August/September. 17 cm.

▼ Sand Martin
Banks and sandy cliffs. Seen
April-September. 12 cm.

◀ House Martin
Suburban areas and
countryside. Seen
April-October.
13 cm.

◀ Swallow
Farms and open country;
often near water. Seen
April-September/October.
19 cm.

**◀ Great Spotted
Woodpecker**
Woodlands. Large
white patches on
wings. 23 cm.

**◀ Green
Woodpecker**
Deciduous woods,
parks. Yellow-green
rump seen in flight.
Rare in Scotland.
32 cm.

**Lesser Spotted
Woodpecker ▶**
Deciduous woods,
parks. Not in
Scotland.
Sparrow-sized.
14 cm.

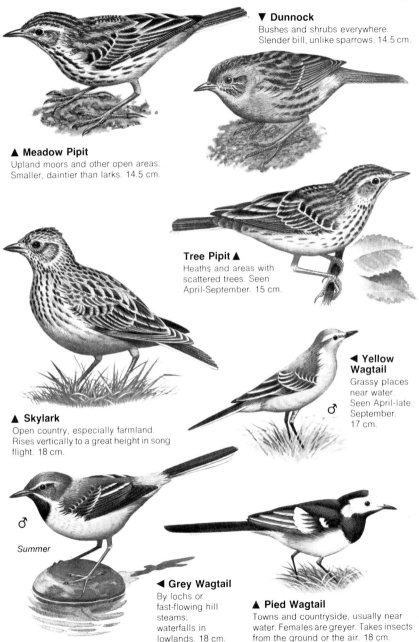

▼ Dunnock
Bushes and shrubs everywhere.
Slender bill, unlike sparrows. 14.5 cm.

▲ Meadow Pipit
Upland moors and other open areas.
Smaller, daintier than larks. 14.5 cm.

Tree Pipit ▲
Heaths and areas with
scattered trees. Seen
April-September. 15 cm.

▲ Skylark
Open country, especially farmland.
Rises vertically to a great height in song
flight. 18 cm.

◄ Yellow Wagtail
Grassy places
near water.
Seen April-late
September.
17 cm.

♂

♂

Summer

◄ Grey Wagtail
By lochs or
fast-flowing hill
steams;
waterfalls in
lowlands. 18 cm.

▲ Pied Wagtail
Towns and countryside, usually near
water. Females are greyer. Takes insects
from the ground or the air. 18 cm.

▼ Willow Warbler
Gardens, woods and hedgerows. Flatter head and longer tail than Chiffchaff. Seen April-September. 11 cm.

▲ Sedge Warbler
Thick vegetation near water. Broad, pale stripe over eye. Seen April-September. 13 cm.

Wren ▶
Towns and countryside. Tiny, rotund bird with cocked tail. 9.5 cm.

Reed Warbler ▼
Reed beds. Not in Scotland. Seen April-September. 13 cm.

♂

♀

▲ Blackcap
Wooded areas. Seen April-September, a few in winter. 14 cm.

▼ Whitethroat
Thick, low bushes. Seen April-September. 14 cm.

▲ Garden Warbler
Hedges or woods with thick undergrowth. Seen April-September. 14 cm.

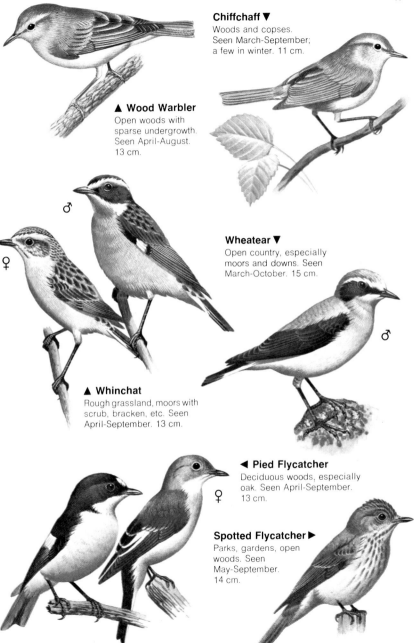

▲ Wood Warbler
Open woods with
sparse undergrowth.
Seen April-August.
13 cm.

Chiffchaff ▼
Woods and copses.
Seen March-September;
a few in winter. 11 cm.

♂

♀

▲ Whinchat
Rough grassland, moors with
scrub, bracken, etc. Seen
April-September. 13 cm.

Wheatear ▼
Open country, especially
moors and downs. Seen
March-October. 15 cm.

♂

◄ Pied Flycatcher
Deciduous woods, especially
oak. Seen April-September.
13 cm.

♀

Spotted Flycatcher ▶
Parks, gardens, open
woods. Seen
May-September.
14 cm.

Blackbird ▼
In trees and bushes everywhere. Young are paler than female with breast more strongly spotted. 25 cm.

♀

♂

▼ Starling
Most places, including cities. In summer, has purple and green gloss and mostly yellow bill. 22 cm.

Juvenile

Adult in winter

▲ Redwing
Farmland, commons and other open areas. A few breed in Scotland. Seen October-April. 21 cm.

◀ Fieldfare
Farmland, orchards, open areas. White underwings. Seen October-April. 25.5 cm.

▼ Redstart
Heaths, parks, open woods. Seen April-September. Rather Robin-like. 14 cm.

♀

♂

Robin ▲
Gardens, hedgerows and woodland. Juvenile is spotted, without any red. 14 cm.

◀ Song Thrush
Trees and bushes in towns and country.
Smashes snails on stones. 23 cm.

Long-tailed Tit ▶
Hedgerows and
woodland edges.
14 cm. (7.5 cm of
which is the tail).

◀ Great Tit
Gardens and
woodlands. Black
band on chest. 14 cm.

◀ Blue Tit
Woods and gardens.
Dark line on belly.
11 cm.

▲ Mistle Thrush
Woodland and open areas.
Larger than Blackbird; paler,
greyer than Song Thrush. 27 cm.

▼ Marsh Tit
Deciduous woods;
infrequently in
gardens. 11 cm.

▲ Coal Tit
Coniferous woods, parks,
gardens. Oblong white patch
on nape. 11 cm.

▼ Chaffinch
Farmland, hedgerows and woodland. Male is duller in winter. White wing bar seen in flight. 15 cm.

♀

♂

♀

♂

Summer

▲ Siskin
Usually coniferous woods in summer; birch, alder woods, sometimes gardens, in winter. 11 cm.

▲ Nuthatch
Deciduous wood and parks. Can descend trees head-first. Very short tail. Rare in Scotland. 14 cm.

▲ Hawfinch
Deciduous woodland, orchards. Very elusive. Big head and massive, broad bill. 16 cm.

◀ Treecreeper
Woodland, sometimes parks and gardens. Creeps up tree trunks using tail as support. 13 cm.

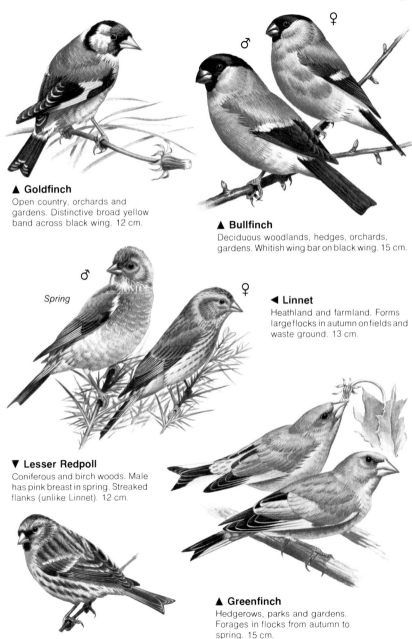

▲ Goldfinch

Open country, orchards and gardens. Distinctive broad yellow band across black wing. 12 cm.

▲ Bullfinch

Deciduous woodlands, hedges, orchards, gardens. Whitish wing bar on black wing. 15 cm.

Spring

◀ Linnet

Heathland and farmland. Forms large flocks in autumn on fields and waste ground. 13 cm.

▼ Lesser Redpoll

Coniferous and birch woods. Male has pink breast in spring. Streaked flanks (unlike Linnet). 12 cm.

▲ Greenfinch

Hedgerows, parks and gardens. Forages in flocks from autumn to spring. 15 cm.

▲ House Sparrow
Near houses in cities; on farms in the country. Distinctive black bib on male. 15 cm.

▼ Tree Sparrow
Farmland. White cheeks with black spot. Sometimes flocks with House Sparrow in winter. 14 cm.

▲ Corn Bunting
Open country, especially cornfields. Bigger than other buntings and finches. 18 cm.

▲ Yellowhammer
Farmland, heaths, young plantations. Flocks forage in fields in winter. Rare in Wales. 17 cm.

▲ Goldcrest
Large gardens and woods, especially conifers. Smallest British bird. 9 cm.

▲ Reed Bunting
Vegetation near water; may visit bird tables in winter. Male has less black on head in winter. 15 cm.

Carrion Crow ▶
Open country, town, along coasts. Usually seen alone, in pairs or small groups. 47 cm.

▼ Jay
Woodlands, parks and gardens. White rump and blue wing flash show in flight. 32 cm.

◀ Magpie
Hedgerows, farmland, scrub. Large black and white bird. Long, slender tail. 46 cm.

▼ Jackdaw
Cliffs, farmland and towns. Small black and grey crow. Forms large flocks. 33 cm.

▲ Rook
Farmland, open copses, villages. Forms large flocks. Baggy thighs. Bare whitish face in adults. 46 cm.

Mammals

▼ Red Fox

Farmland and woods, sometimes mountains and towns. Mainly nocturnal. 65 cm.

▲ Badger

Woods, sometimes mountains. Nocturnal. Can stay underground for several days in cold weather without food. 80 cm.

▼ Roe Deer

Conifer plantations, especially near water. Mainly nocturnal; hides during day. 70 cm.

▲ Hedgehog

Hedgerows, ditches, parks, gardens and moorland. Mainly nocturnal. 25 cm.

▲ Mole

Underground in most kinds of soil in farmland, woods. Lives alone. Can swim well. 13 cm.

▼ Grey Squirrel
Woods, parks and gardens.
Introduced from N. America.
Diurnal. 27 cm.

Red Squirrel ▲
Mainly conifer woods. Partly replaced
by Grey Squirrel in England. 23 cm.

▼ Rabbit
Farmland, woodland, sand
dunes and hillsides. Active
at dusk and dawn. 40 cm.

◄ Brown Hare
Open farmland and
woodland. Mainly
nocturnal, but can often be
seen in day. 58 cm.

▼ Wood Mouse
Gardens,
hedgerows,
woods. Mainly
nocturnal. 9 cm.

▼ Common Shrew
Rough pasture, woods,
hedgerows, dunes and
marshes. Active day and
night. 7 cm.

▼ Short-tailed Vole
Open ground with
rough grass. Most
active at night; also
seen in day. 11 cm.

◄ Grey Seal
Rocky shores, mainly along
Atlantic coast; some on east coast
of Scotland and north-east coast of
England. 3 m.

Common Seal ►
Flat shores, estuaries and
mudbanks on Scottish coasts and
mainly east coast of England.
Blunter head than Grey Seal.
1.5 m.

◄ Stoat
Woods, farmland,
mountains. Tip of
tail always black. Mainly
nocturnal. 28 cm.

▲ Weasel
Same habitat as Stoat,
but prefers dry places.
Mainly nocturnal.
20 cm.

Water Vole ►
Ponds, canals, streams and
marshes. Mainly diurnal.
May also be black. 19 cm.

Otter ►
Alongside rivers, lakes;
marshes, coasts and the sea.
Nocturnal. More common in
Scotland. 70 cm.

Wild Flowers

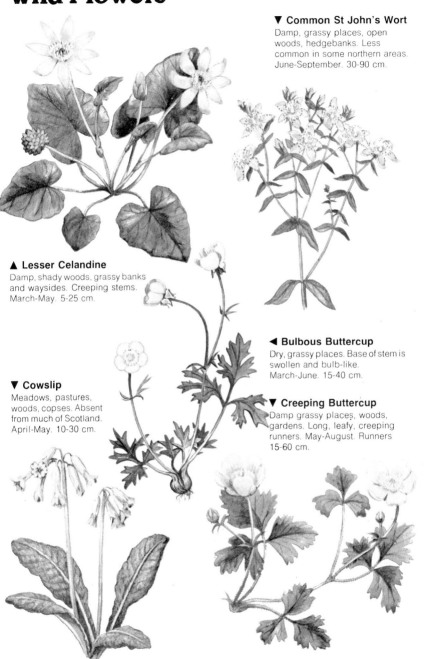

▼ Common St John's Wort
Damp, grassy places, open woods, hedgebanks. Less common in some northern areas. June-September. 30-90 cm.

▲ Lesser Celandine
Damp, shady woods, grassy banks and waysides. Creeping stems. March-May. 5-25 cm.

◄ Bulbous Buttercup
Dry, grassy places. Base of stem is swollen and bulb-like. March-June. 15-40 cm.

▼ Cowslip
Meadows, pastures, woods, copses. Absent from much of Scotland. April-May. 10-30 cm.

▼ Creeping Buttercup
Damp grassy places, woods, gardens. Long, leafy, creeping runners. May-August. Runners 15-60 cm.

▼ Creeping Jenny
Grassy, shady places; damp meadows, woods, under hedges. Rare in northern Scotland. June-August. Stems up to 60 cm.

◄ Yellow Rattle
Waysides and other grassy places. Seeds rattle inside ripe capsule. May-August. 12-40 cm.

Common Rockrose ▶
Grassy, rocky places. Not a rose. Leaves are hairy. May-September 5-30 cm.

Aaron's Rod ▶
Banks, waste places, open scrub. Rarer in Scotland. June-August. 30-200 cm.

◄ Groundsel
Waste places; a
common garden weed.
Flowers all year round.
8-45 cm.

▲ Primrose
Woods, hedges and fields. Rarer
in the North. February-May.
8-15 cm.

◄ Herb Bennet
Woods, hedges, shady places.
Fruits are hooked. June-August.
20-60 cm.

◄ Broom
Heaths, waste ground,
open woods,
scrubland. May-June.
60-200 cm.

▲ Yellow Pimpernel
Woods and shady
hedgebanks. May-September.
Trailing stems up to 40 cm long.

◄ Silverweed
Hedgebanks, grassy places. Creeping stems. May-August.

Fruits (in autumn)

▲ Old Man's Beard
Woodland edges, hedgerows, scrub. Rare in Scotland and northern England. July-August. Up to 30 m.

▼ Bird's Foot Trefoil
Open, grassy places. Very long, creeping stems. Pods look like a bird's foot. May-June.

Golden Rod ►
Woods, cliffs, hedges. Rarer in the South-East. July-September. 5-75 cm.

▼ Creeping Cinquefoil
Hedgebanks, grassy places. Creeping stems. May-August.

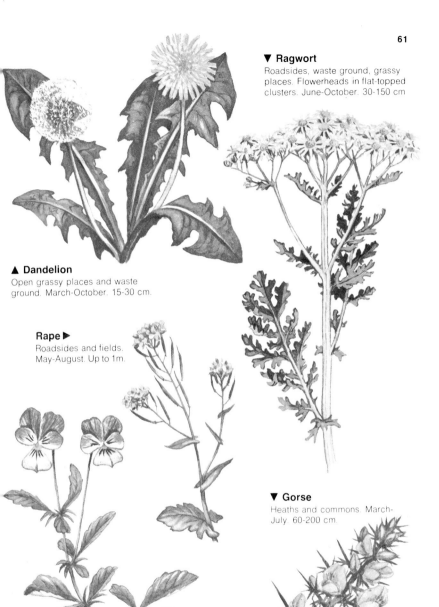

▼ Ragwort
Roadsides, waste ground, grassy places. Flowerheads in flat-topped clusters. June-October. 30-150 cm

▲ Dandelion
Open grassy places and waste ground. March-October. 15-30 cm.

Rape ▶
Roadsides and fields. May-August. Up to 1m.

▼ Gorse
Heaths and commons. March-July. 60-200 cm.

▲ Wild Pansy
Grassy places and cornfields. Flowers can also be all yellow, all violet, or pink and white. April-September. 15-45 cm.

▼ Viper's Bugloss
Waysides and sand dunes. Sharp
hairs on stems. Bristly leaves. Rare in
Scotland. June-September. 30-90 cm.

Common
Forget-me-Not ▶
Roadsides, fields, and
open grassy places.
April-September.
15-30 cm.

◀ Sea Aster
Saltmarshes. Petals can
also be white.
July-October. 1 m.

◀ Common
Speedwell
Grassy places and
woods. May-August.
10-40 cm.

Common Milkwort ▶
Heaths, dunes, grassy
places. May-September.
10-30 cm.

▼ Brooklime
In and by ponds, streams and other wet places. May-September. 20-60 cm.

Lesser Periwinkle ▶
Woods and hedgebanks. March-May. Flowering stems up to 15 cm.

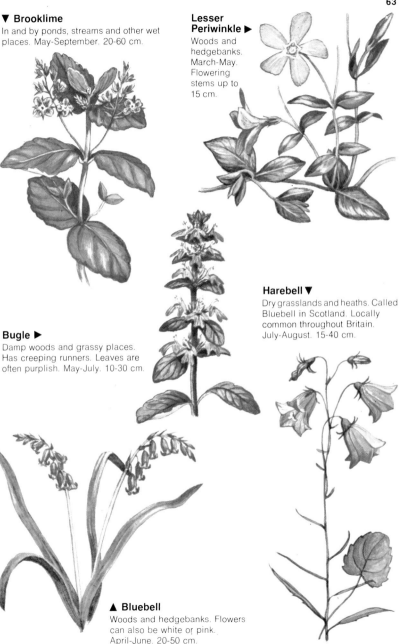

Harebell ▼
Dry grasslands and heaths. Called Bluebell in Scotland. Locally common throughout Britain. July-August. 15-40 cm.

Bugle ▶
Damp woods and grassy places. Has creeping runners. Leaves are often purplish. May-July. 10-30 cm.

▲ Bluebell
Woods and hedgebanks. Flowers can also be white or pink. April-June. 20-50 cm.

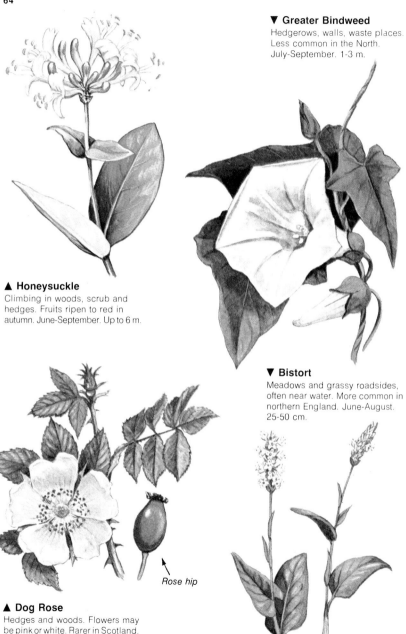

▼ Greater Bindweed
Hedgerows, walls, waste places.
Less common in the North.
July-September. 1-3 m.

▲ Honeysuckle
Climbing in woods, scrub and
hedges. Fruits ripen to red in
autumn. June-September. Up to 6 m.

▼ Bistort
Meadows and grassy roadsides,
often near water. More common in
northern England. June-August.
25-50 cm.

Rose hip

▲ Dog Rose
Hedges and woods. Flowers may
be pink or white. Rarer in Scotland.
June-July. 1-3 m.

▼ Knotgrass
Waste ground, fields and seashores. A low, far-spreading plant. July-October. Creeping stems 3-200 cm.

Great Willowherb ▶
Ditches, marshes, near streams. Rare in northern Scotland. July-August. 80-150 cm.

◀ Sea Bindweed
Sandy beaches; sometimes shingle. Rare in Scotland. June-August. Trailing stems up to 50 cm.

▼ Sand Spurrey
Sandy or gravelly places. Leaves end in a small bristle. May-September. 5-25 cm.

▲ Sea Milkwort
Grassy saltmarshes. Creeping stems. June-August. 10-30 cm tall.

◀ Thrift
Rocky cliffs near coast; mountains inland. March-October. 5-30 cm.

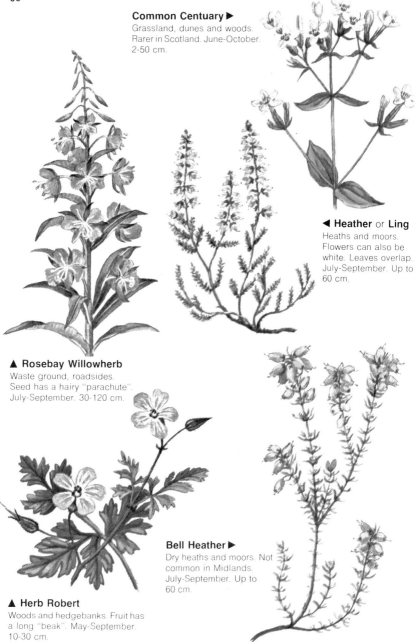

Common Centuary ▶
Grassland, dunes and woods.
Rarer in Scotland. June-October.
2-50 cm.

◀ Heather or **Ling**
Heaths and moors.
Flowers can also be
white. Leaves overlap.
July-September. Up to
60 cm.

▲ Rosebay Willowherb
Waste ground, roadsides.
Seed has a hairy "parachute".
July-September. 30-120 cm.

Bell Heather ▶
Dry heaths and moors. Not
common in Midlands.
July-September. Up to
60 cm.

▲ Herb Robert
Woods and hedgebanks. Fruit has
a long "beak". May-September.
10-30 cm.

▼ Bilberry
Heaths, moors and woods.
Blue-black berries. Flowers
April-June. Up to 60 cm.

Ragged Robin ▲
Damp meadows,
marshes, woods. Sepals
form a tube. May-June.
30-75 cm.

Lady's Smock ▼
Damp meadows and near streams.
Flower can be pink or white and
lilac. April-June. 15-60 cm.

▲ Lesser Knapweed
Grassland and waysides. Stem is
grooved below flowerhead.
June-September. 15-60 cm.

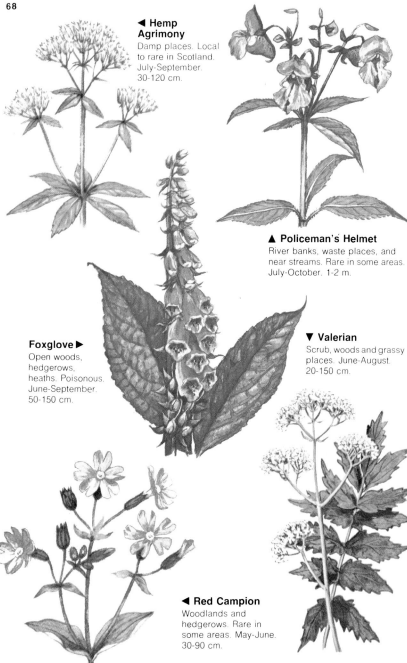

◀ Hemp Agrimony
Damp places. Local to rare in Scotland. July-September. 30-120 cm.

▲ Policeman's Helmet
River banks, waste places, and near streams. Rare in some areas. July-October. 1-2 m.

Foxglove ▶
Open woods, hedgerows, heaths. Poisonous. June-September. 50-150 cm.

▼ Valerian
Scrub, woods and grassy places. June-August. 20-150 cm.

◀ Red Campion
Woodlands and hedgerows. Rare in some areas. May-June. 30-90 cm.

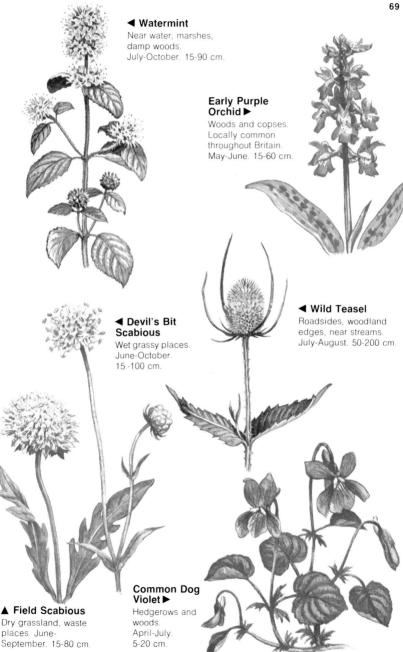

◄ Watermint
Near water, marshes,
damp woods.
July-October. 15-90 cm.

**Early Purple
Orchid ►**
Woods and copses.
Locally common
throughout Britain.
May-June. 15-60 cm.

**◄ Devil's Bit
Scabious**
Wet grassy places.
June-October.
15-100 cm.

◄ Wild Teasel
Roadsides, woodland
edges, near streams.
July-August. 50-200 cm.

▲ Field Scabious
Dry grassland, waste
places. June-
September. 15-80 cm.

**Common Dog
Violet ►**
Hedgerows and
woods.
April-July.
5-20 cm.

Tufted Vetch ▼
Climbs on other plants in hedges
and grassy places. June-August.
Flowers 10 mm long.

▲ Ivy-leaved Toadflax
Old walls, occasionally rocks.
Often forms clumps. May-September.
Flowers 10 mm long.

Sea Lavender ▼
Muddy saltmarshes. Often forms
large mats. Not in northern
Scotland. July-October. 8-30 cm.

▲ Woody Nightshade
Hedges, woods, waste places. Poisonous.
Not common in Scotland. June-September.
Scrambling stems 30-200 cm.

▼ Long-headed Poppy
Corn and other fields and waste ground. Longer capsule and paler petals than Field Poppy. June-July. 20-60 cm.

Capsule

▲ Scarlet Pimpernel
Cultivated and waste ground. A sub-species has small blue flowers. Rarer in Scotland. June-August. 6-30 cm.

◄ Field Poppy
Corn and other fields, waste ground. Rare in northern Scotland. June-August. 20-60 cm.

Capsule

▼ Wood Woundwort
Woods, hedgebanks, waste ground. July-August. 30-100 cm.

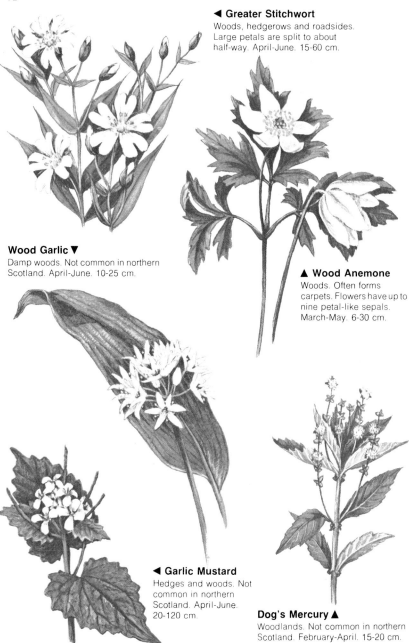

◀ Greater Stitchwort
Woods, hedgerows and roadsides. Large petals are split to about half-way. April-June. 15-60 cm.

Wood Garlic ▼
Damp woods. Not common in northern Scotland. April-June. 10-25 cm.

▲ Wood Anemone
Woods. Often forms carpets. Flowers have up to nine petal-like sepals. March-May. 6-30 cm.

◀ Garlic Mustard
Hedges and woods. Not common in northern Scotland. April-June. 20-120 cm.

Dog's Mercury ▲
Woodlands. Not common in northern Scotland. February-April. 15-20 cm.

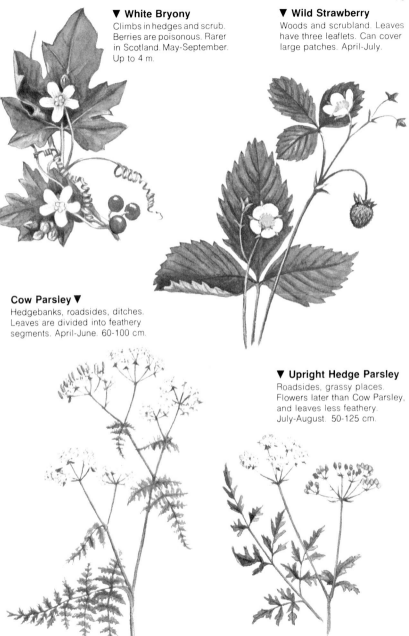

▼ White Bryony
Climbs in hedges and scrub. Berries are poisonous. Rarer in Scotland. May-September. Up to 4 m.

▼ Wild Strawberry
Woods and scrubland. Leaves have three leaflets. Can cover large patches. April-July.

Cow Parsley ▼
Hedgebanks, roadsides, ditches. Leaves are divided into feathery segments. April-June. 60-100 cm.

▼ Upright Hedge Parsley
Roadsides, grassy places. Flowers later than Cow Parsley, and leaves less feathery. July-August. 50-125 cm.

74

▼ Meadowsweet
Marshes, water meadows and near ditches. Flowers smell sweet.
May-September. 60-120 cm.

▲ Water Crowfoot
Ponds, streams and ditches. May-June.
Flowers are 10-20 mm across.

Wild Carrot ▶
Grassy places, especially near the sea. June-August. 30-100 cm.

Hogweed ▲
Open woods, roadsides, grassy places.
June-September.
50-200 cm.

Daisy ▲
Short grassland, especially lawns.
March-October. 3-12 cm.

▲ Nettle

Waysides, waste ground, woods. Has stinging hairs. June-August. 30-150 cm.

▼ White Dead Nettle

Roadsides, hedgerows and waste ground. Rare in north Scotland. May-December. 20-60 cm.

▼ White Clover

Garden lawns, grassy places. June-September. Upright stems up to 25 cm.

▲ Shepherd's Purse

Waysides and waste ground. Flowers all year. 3-40 cm.

◄ White Campion
Waysides, hedgebanks, waste ground. Sticky hairs. May-September. 30-100 cm.

◄ Bladder Campion
Roadsides and grassy places. Usually hairless. June-August. 25-90 cm.

◄ Sea Campion
Sea cliffs, shingle beaches. Smaller than Bladder Campion, with broader petals. June-August. 8-25 cm.

▼ Chickweed
Fields, waste places, gardens. Flowers all year. 5-40 cm.

▲ Corn Spurrey
Cornfields, cultivated land. June-August. 7-40 cm.

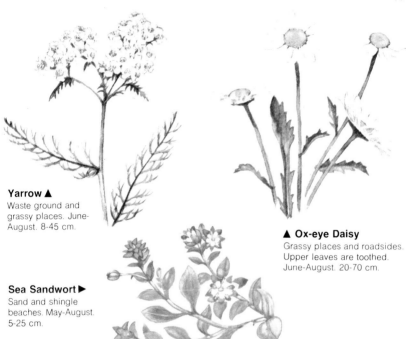

Yarrow ▲
Waste ground and
grassy places. June-
August. 8-45 cm.

▲ Ox-eye Daisy
Grassy places and roadsides.
Upper leaves are toothed.
June-August. 20-70 cm.

Sea Sandwort ▶
Sand and shingle
beaches. May-August.
5-25 cm.

▼ Pellitory-of-the-wall
Wall and rock crevices. Not in
northern Scotland. June-October.
30-100 cm.

▲ Wood Sorrel
Woods and hedgebanks. Flowers
close at night and in bad weather.
Petals have lilac veins. April-May. 5-15 cm.

78

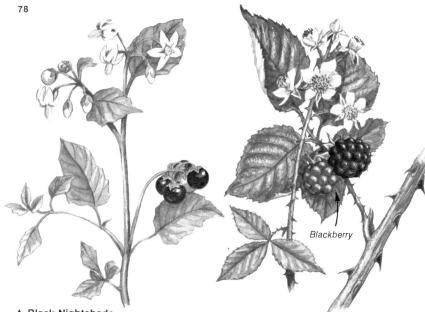

Blackberry

▲ Black Nightshade
Cultivated and waste ground. Rare in
Scotland. July-September. Up to 60 cm.

▲ Bramble
Woods, scrubland, hedges, open
ground. May-September. Arching
stems up to 5 m.

▼ Greater Plantain
Cultivated land, waysides,
lawns. Broad leaves.
May-September. 10-15 cm.

▲ Ribwort Plantain
Grassy and waste places, lawns.
Ribbed leaves. April-August.
Up to 45 cm.

Butterflies

Wall Brown ♂

▲ **Wall Brown**
Woodlands and rough, open ground. Often rests on walls. Not in northern Scotland. Seen March-September. 44-46 mm.

Grayling ♀

▲ **Grayling**
Sandy places, chalk downs. Less common in Wales and East Anglia. Seen July-August. 56-61 mm.

Meadow Brown ♀

▲ **Meadow Brown**
Meadows and other grassy places. Less common in Scotland. Seen June-September. 50-55 mm.

Small Heath ▶
Many areas including open woods, marshes and dry hillsides. Seen April-September. 33-35 mm.

Painted Lady ▶
Dry, open places. Likes
thistles. Seen
June-October. 62-65 mm.

Painted Lady

Red Admiral ▶
Gardens and woodland edges.
Migrant from North Africa. Seen
May-October. 66-68 mm.

▲ Small Tortoiseshell
Gardens and open places. Less
widespread in Wales and
Scotland. Seen April-November.
48-52 mm.
▼

*Small
Tortoiseshell*

▲ Peacock
Gardens. Not present in northern Scotland.
Seen August-October. 62-68 mm.

▲ Orange Tip
Woodland edges and hedgerows. Not in parts of Scotland. Seen April-June. 42-48 mm.
▼

Orange Tip

▲ Common Blue
Prefers downs and rough meadows. Seen April-September. 28-36 mm.

Common Blue

▼ Small Copper
All types of country. Less widespread in Scotland. Seen May-September. 26-30 mm.

Caterpillar of Small Copper

▲ Large White
Woods, gardens and open places. Caterpillar eats brassicas. Seen May-August. 62-64 mm.

Large White ♀

♀

▲ Brimstone
Hedges, gardens and woodland paths. Adult hibernates. Not in Scotland. Seen June-September. 58-60 mm.

Brimstone ♂

▼ Small White
Gardens and other cultivated places. Less widespread in Scotland. Seen May-August. 48-50 mm.

▼ Green-veined White
Open woodland and grassy places, gardens. Caterpillar eats leaves and seed-pods of Garlic Mustard. Seen May-September. 47-50 mm.

Seashore

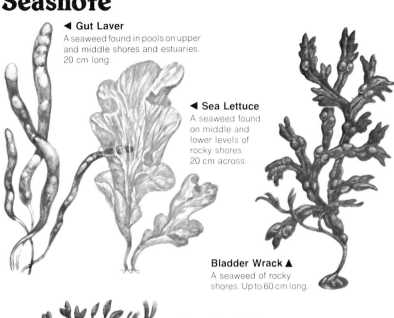

◄ Gut Laver
A seaweed found in pools on upper and middle shores and estuaries. 20 cm long.

◄ Sea Lettuce
A seaweed found on middle and lower levels of rocky shores. 20 cm across.

Bladder Wrack ▲
A seaweed of rocky shores. Up to 60 cm long.

◄ Channelled Wrack
A seaweed found on rocks of the upper shore. 10 cm tall.

▼ Bread-crumb Sponge
On rocks, shells and seaweed holdfasts. 10 cm across.

▲ Haliclona oculata
A sponge found on lower shores in fast currents and estuaries with muddy gravel. Up to 16 cm long.

Sea Oak ►
A seaweed found in pools, on stalks of other seaweeds and on rocks. 20 cm tall.

▼ Beadlet Anemone
Rock pools at most levels of the shore. 5 cm high.

▼ Snakelocks Anemone
Rocky shores. Not on east or south-east coasts. Can be grey or greenish. 10 cm across.

▲ Daisy Anemone
In rock crevices or mud of shallow pools. 10 cm high.

Dahlia Anemone

▲ Dahlia Anemone
In crevices in rock pools. 15 cm high when open.

◄ Hermit Crab Anemone
On mollusc shells inhabited by Hermit Crab. 10 cm high.

◄ Common Hermit Crab
Mostly lower shore, in rock pools. 5-10 cm long.

▲ Common Limpet
On rocky shores, attached to rocks. 7 cm long.

▲ Common Periwinkle
On rocky and muddy shores. 2.5 cm high.

▲ Netted Dog Whelk
On mud and gravel off shore and on lower shore. 2.5 cm high.

▲ Saddle Oyster
On lower shore, attached to rocks. 6 cm wide.

▲ Common Whelk
Lower shore of rocky or sandy beaches. 8 cm high.

▲ Slipper Limpet
Low water and off shore, often attached to one another. 4-5 cm long.

▲ Common Mussel
Rocky shores, pier piles and estuaries. 1-10 cm long.

▲ Dog Whelk
On rocks and in crevices of lower shore. 3 cm high.

▲ Painted Topshell
On rocks and under stones on lower shore. 2.5 cm high.

▲ Common Oyster
Shallow and deep water. 10-15 cm long.

▲ Necklace Shell
Sandy shores. 3 cm high.

▲ Rayed Trough Shell
Sand or gravel on lower shores. 5 cm long.

▲ Razor Shell
Burrows in mud. 12 cm long.

▲ Baltic Tellin
In mud and sand of seashores and estuaries.
2 cm long.

▲ Common Sand Gaper
Burrows in muddy sand on lower shore.
12 cm wide.

▲ Horse Mussel
From lower shore to deep water. 20 cm long.

▲ Edible Cockle
In mud and sand of middle shore and below.
4 cm across.

▲ Flat Periwinkle
Under brown seaweed on rocky shores.
1 cm high.

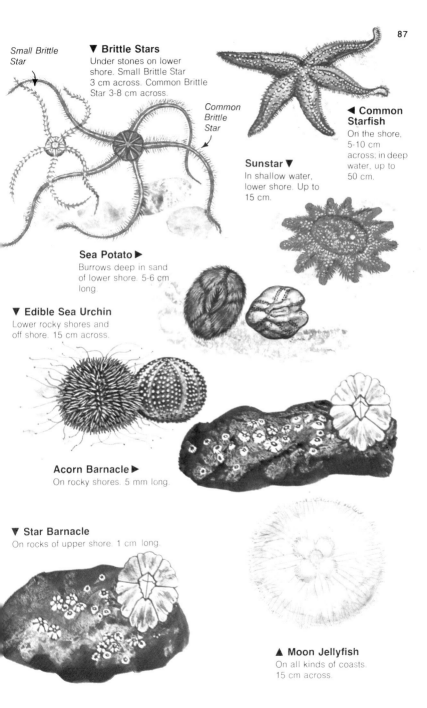

Small Brittle Star

▼ Brittle Stars
Under stones on lower shore. Small Brittle Star 3 cm across. Common Brittle Star 3-8 cm across.

Common Brittle Star

◄ Common Starfish
On the shore, 5-10 cm across; in deep water, up to 50 cm.

Sunstar ▼
In shallow water, lower shore. Up to 15 cm.

Sea Potato ►
Burrows deep in sand of lower shore. 5-6 cm long.

▼ Edible Sea Urchin
Lower rocky shores and off shore. 15 cm across.

Acorn Barnacle ►
On rocky shores. 5 mm long.

▼ Star Barnacle
On rocks of upper shore. 1 cm long.

▲ Moon Jellyfish
On all kinds of coasts. 15 cm across.

▲ Common Prawn
Shallow water and rock pools. 5-8 cm long.

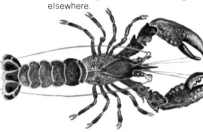

▼ Common Lobster
Only small ones in rock pools of lower shore. Can grow up to 45 cm long elsewhere.

▲ White Shrimp
Rock pools on lower shore; shallow waters of estuaries. 5 cm long.

▼ Montagu's Plated Lobster
Under seaweed and stones of lower shore. 4-6 cm long.

▲ Sand Shrimp
Sand estuaries. 5 cm long.

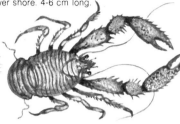

▼ Edible Crab
Only small ones in rock pools in lower shore. Can grow up to 11.5 cm long elsewhere.

▲ Shore Crab
Sandy, muddy and rocky shores; estuaries. 8 cm across.

▲ Broad-clawed Porcelain Crab
Under stones on middle and lower shores. 1.2 cm across.

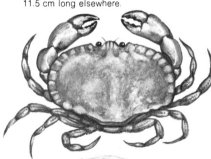

Cuttlebone

▲ Common Cuttlefish
In sheltered bays and washed up dead on strand line. 30 cm long.

Trees

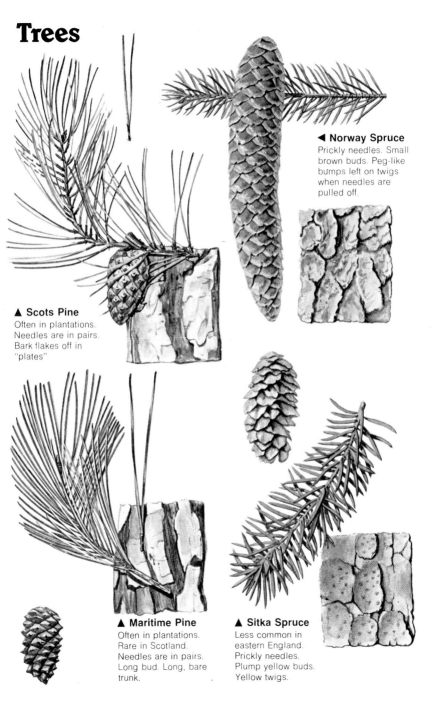

◄ Norway Spruce
Prickly needles. Small brown buds. Peg-like bumps left on twigs when needles are pulled off.

▲ Scots Pine
Often in plantations. Needles are in pairs. Bark flakes off in "plates"

▲ Maritime Pine
Often in plantations. Rare in Scotland. Needles are in pairs. Long bud. Long, bare trunk.

▲ Sitka Spruce
Less common in eastern England. Prickly needles. Plump yellow buds. Yellow twigs.

▼ European Larch

Deciduous. Bunches of soft, light green needles leave small knobs on twigs when they fall.

▲ Douglas Fir

Soft, fragrant needles. Cones have three-pointed bracts on each scale.

▼ European Silver Fir

Rare in east and south-east England. Needles are green above, silvery below.

▲ Corsican Pine

Often in plantations. Needles are in pairs. Onion-shaped buds.

Cone

▼ Yew
Often planted in churchyards.
Leaves and berries are poisonous.

▲ Juniper
Needles are in threes
with white band on
upper surface.
Berry-like cones.

▼ English Oak
Less common in
northern Scotland.
Acorns have long
stalks. Leaves are
short-stalked.

Acorn

▲ Chile Pine
Also called Monkey Puzzle. Stiff,
leathery leaves with sharp points.

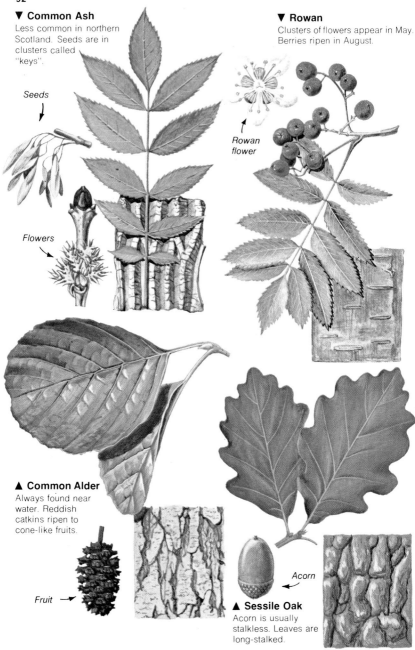

▼ Common Ash
Less common in northern Scotland. Seeds are in clusters called "keys".

Seeds

Flowers

▼ Rowan
Clusters of flowers appear in May. Berries ripen in August.

Rowan flower

▲ Common Alder
Always found near water. Reddish catkins ripen to cone-like fruits.

Fruit →

▲ Sessile Oak
Acorn is usually stalkless. Leaves are long-stalked.

Acorn

▼ Aspen
Often grows in thickets. Leaves tremble in the wind. White downy catkins appear in May on female trees.

Catkin

▲ Goat Willow
Common on damp waste ground and in scrub woodland. Catkins, known as Pussy Willows, appear in late winter.

▼ White Willow
Common by water. Not in north-west Scotland. Weeping Willow is a variety of this species.

Catkin

▲ Silver Birch
Catkins, known as "lamb's tails", are yellow with pollen in April. Bark peels off in ribbons.

Catkin

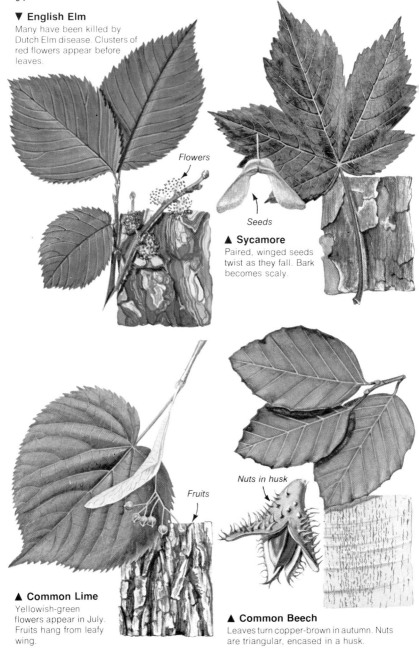

▼ English Elm
Many have been killed by Dutch Elm disease. Clusters of red flowers appear before leaves.

Flowers

Seeds

▲ Sycamore
Paired, winged seeds twist as they fall. Bark becomes scaly.

Fruits

▲ Common Lime
Yellowish-green flowers appear in July. Fruits hang from leafy wing.

Nuts in husk

▲ Common Beech
Leaves turn copper-brown in autumn. Nuts are triangular, encased in a husk.

▼ Sweet Chestnut
Flowers appear in June. Edible chestnuts are encased in a prickly fruit.

Flowers

Fruits

▲ Horse Chestnut
Less common in Scotland. "Candles" of flowers (white or pink) appear in May.

▲ Holly
Less common in northern Scotland. Evergreen. Berries found only on female trees.

Flowers

▲ Common Hawthorn
Grows in thickets and hedgerows. Berries usually have only one stone.

The leaves and bark of each of the species shown below are illustrated on page 89–95.

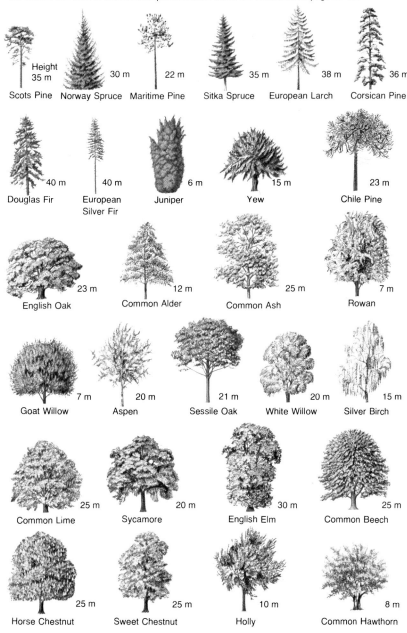

Height
35 m — Scots Pine

30 m — Norway Spruce

22 m — Maritime Pine

35 m — Sitka Spruce

38 m — European Larch

36 m — Corsican Pine

40 m — Douglas Fir

40 m — European Silver Fir

6 m — Juniper

15 m — Yew

23 m — Chile Pine

23 m — English Oak

12 m — Common Alder

25 m — Common Ash

7 m — Rowan

7 m — Goat Willow

20 m — Aspen

21 m — Sessile Oak

20 m — White Willow

15 m — Silver Birch

25 m — Common Lime

20 m — Sycamore

30 m — English Elm

25 m — Common Beech

25 m — Horse Chestnut

25 m — Sweet Chestnut

10 m — Holly

8 m — Common Hawthorn

Places to Visit

This section describes a selection of places to visit to observe wildlife. They range from nature reserves, wildfowl refuges and good birdwatching areas to zoos, wildlife parks, country parks, gardens and museums. Much of Scotland's wild coast ne, and many of its moors and mountains are interesting for their wildlife, and the sites selected are mainly those which have reasonable interpretation facilities and are fairly easily accessed.

A map of Scotland on the following pages (98–101) shows the regions and the places to visit (marked by number). The descriptions that follow are grouped under Region and the entries are listed alphabetically, with the entry number shown on the map.

The descriptions outline the main points of interest in each place. They also give details about location, approach by road, and restrictions on opening times. For places outside towns, the Ordnance Survey (1:50 000) map number and grid reference is given, at the very end of each description (eg. OS 142: 205 890). The sheet number follows after "OS" and the grid reference after the colon. With large areas, such as forests and estuaries, a square reference (eg. OS 142: 20 89) is given for the approximate centre of the area. The reference for small gardens sometimes indicates the nearest village.

In case of nature reserves and wildfowl refuges, the organization which owns or leases them is cited at the beginning of the description. In some, public access is restricted in order to protect the habitat and its wildlife, and a permit must be obtained in advance. This is indicated where it applies together with details of where to apply for permission. Ranger Services are available in some areas, and these are also indicated: Scotland's countryside rangers provide advice and organize walks and trails for visitors.

The visitor to nature reserves is reminded that the reserve exists to protect the habitat and its wildlife. Great care should therefore be taken on reserves, and any conditions and restrictions on access should be strictly adhered to. (See also the Country Code and points on nature conservation on page 121.)

The Scottish Tourist Board publishes a good range of literature, obtainable from its London, Edinburgh and Scottish Regional Tourist Offices (see page 123). Tourist Information Centres are found in most towns, particularly during the summer months, and these provide both literature and details of opening times for local places of interest. For some places such as private gardens opening times can be irregular and are worth checking in advance. Other useful addresses for organizations such as the RSPB and Nature Conservancy Council are given on page 123.

NB: Caution should be taken when visiting moorlands and forests during the autumn when deer culling and grouse shooting take place.

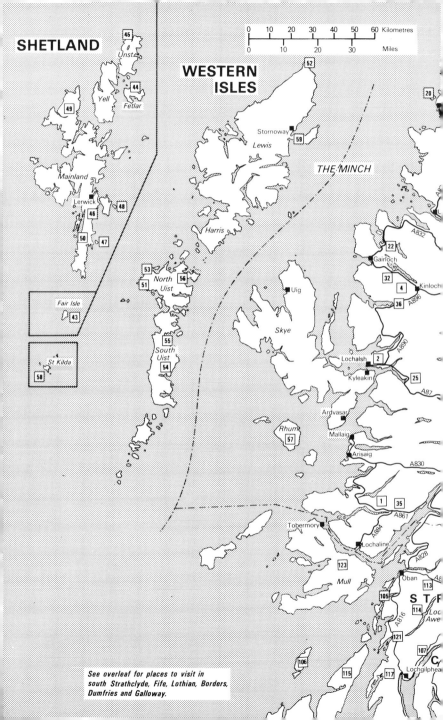

SHETLAND

45 Unst

44 Fetlar

Yell

49

Mainland

48

Lerwick

46

50

47

Fair Isle

43

St Kilda

58

WESTERN ISLES

52

Stornoway **59**

Lewis

THE MINCH

20

A832

22

Gairloch

32

4 Kinloch

36 A896

53 North Uist **56**

51

Uig

55

South Uist **54**

Skye

Lochalsh **2**

A890

Kyleakin

25

A87

Ardvasar

Rhum **57**

Mallaig

Arisaig

A830

1 **35**

A861

Tobermory

A848

Lochaline

A828

123

Mull

Oban

105

S T F

113

114 *Loch Awe*

A816

121

107 C

Lochgilphea

106

115

117

See overleaf for places to visit in south Strathclyde, Fife, Lothian, Borders, Dumfries and Galloway.

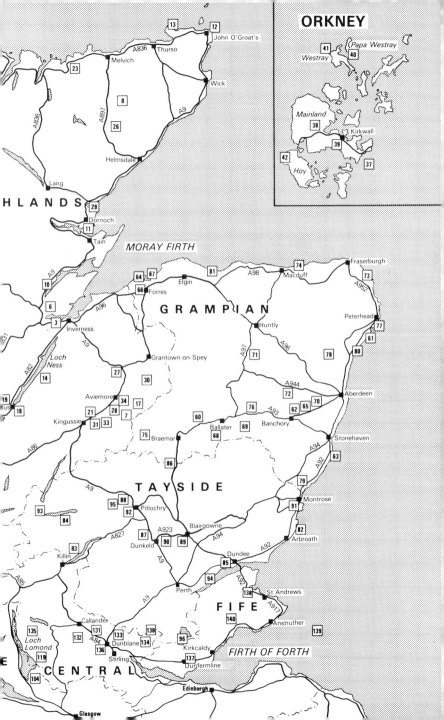

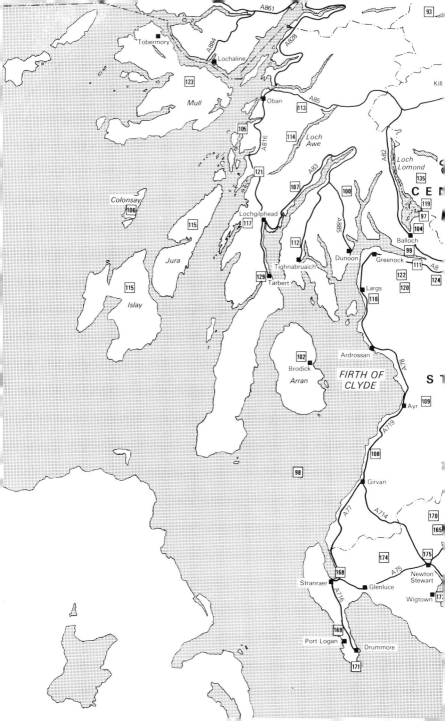

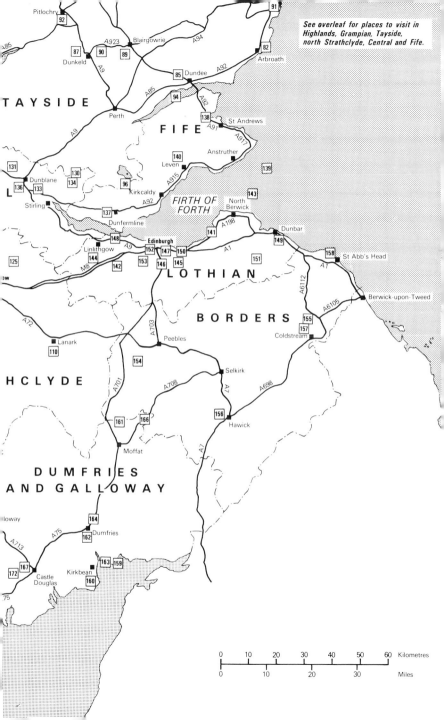

See overleaf for places to visit in Highlands, Grampian, Tayside, north Strathclyde, Central and Fife.

Highlands

1 Arriundle Oakwood
National Nature Reserve

Nature Conservancy Council. Coppice oakwood with rich growth of lichens, liverworts and mosses in the Strontian river valley. Other fine examples of lichen-rich woodlands occur close to the A861 on shore of Loch Sunart.
☐ 30 miles/48 km south-west of Fort William off A861. OS 40: 81 61.

2 Balmacara Estate

National Trust for Scotland. Estate covers most of the Kyle/Plockton peninsula. Habitats vary from moorland and lochans to the shoreline of a sea loch. Walks in woodland gardens by Lochalsh House (not open). Natural history display in Coach House. Ranger Service.
☐ (Tel: Balmacara 278). Lochalsh woodland gardens open all year. Coach House open Easter–mid-October daily. Off A87, Kyle of Lochalsh. OS 33: 95 21.

3 Beauly Firth

Fine views of saltmarsh and mud banks in this estuary rich in Pink-footed and Greylag Geese, Wigeon, Pintail, Redbreasted Merganser, Goosander and waders in spring but offering some interest all year.
☐ Several good vantage points along the A9 between Inverness and Beauly. Parking in lay-bys. OS 26: 52 46.

4 Beinn Eighe
National Nature Reserve

Nature Conservancy Council. The first national nature reserve in Britain. Caledonian pinewood, alpine plant communities, geological interest. Birds include Snow Bunting, Golden Eagle, Ptarmigan, Crossbill. Rare animals include Pine Marten and Wild Cat. Nature trails.
☐ Tourist Information Office at Kinlochewe. Nature trail and Visitor Centre at Aulroy Cottage on A832 north-west of Kinlochewe. (Tel: Kinlochewe 244/254). Reserve is west of the A382/A896 junction close to Kinlochewe. OS 19: 02 62.

5 Ben Nevis

High mountain cliffs and scree. Walks to summit of Britain's highest mountain (4406 ft/1344 m), suitable for well-equipped hill walkers.
☐ Mountain area south-east of Fort William approached on A82. OS 41: 12 72.

6 Black Isle Walks

Wide variety of walks with wildlife interests on the Black Isle between Cromarty Firth and Moray Firth. Wildfowl and waders. Woodland. Uplands. Coastal walks.
☐ Contact Information Centre, Muir of Ord. (Tel: Muir of Ord 433/525). Open all year. On A9, 13 miles/20.5 km north-west of Inverness. OS 26: 52 50.

7 Cairngorm Mountains,
part National Nature Reserve

Nature Conservancy Council. Extensive mountain plateau over 4300 ft/1300 m high with the most "arctic" climate in Britain. Special plant communities adapted to cold conditions in areas of long snow lie. Mountain heath and moorland. Pine woodland. Birch scrub bogs. Rich site for mountain plants. Upland birds include Golden Eagle, Ptarmigan, Snow Bunting. Mammals include Red Deer and Wild Cat. See also Loch-an-Eilein.
☐ Access to area unrestricted except when deer culling may be taking place in autumn. (Tel: Aviemore 810477). Off A9 at Aviemore via A951 past Loch Morlich to car park. OS 36: 98 06.

8 Caithness Flows

One of the largest areas of bog in Britain with an almost continuous cover of peat soils. Of special interest to those wishing to study undisturbed and actively growing peat bogs with characteristic plants and animals. Area contains a complex of moors, bogs, pools and lochs in the catchment of the River Thurso and is bounded by more peatlands.
☐ Between Forsinard Hotel (railway station) on A897 and Altnabreac railway station on minor road off B890 at Westerdale. This route is 15 miles/24 km off the main road and suitable for planned journeys only. OS 11: 00 45.

9 Corrieshalloch Gorge

National Trust for Scotland. Spectacular wooded gorge with high waterfall (Falls of Measach). Views along gorge from suspension bridge. Almost vertical face of gorge (200 ft/60 m) has damp woodland in places with Birch, Rowan, Oak, Hazel and Pine amongst the tree species. Ground flora includes many woodland and some alpine plants with several rare species. Liverworts and mosses are of special interest. Woodland birds and insects. Steep gorge: keep to footpaths.

□ 12 miles/19 km south-east of Ullapool on A835, turn off at Braemore Forest. OS 20: 20 78.

10 Cromarty Firth/Nigg Bay, part National Nature Reserve

Nature Conservancy Council. Internationally important estuary for overwintering wildfowl and waders. Whooper Swan, Mute Swan, Wigeon, Goldeneye, Pintail, Shelduck, Scaup, Oystercatcher, Knot, Curlew, Dunlin, Lapwing, Bar-tailed Godwit, Ringed Plover and Turnstone. Industrial development threatens the ornithological value of this estuary.

□ North of Inverness, along A9 from Dingwall to Alness and along B817 from Alness to Milton. OS 21: 65 69.

11 Dornoch Firth

Outstanding wildlife site with a wide range of estuarine habitats. At Morrich More (north of Tain) lies one of the finest dune systems in Europe. (No access to north end which is used as military range.) Many dune plant species including several at their northern limits. Large Arctic Tern colony. Inland, Loch Eye holds many species of wildfowl in winter. Birds to be seen on the shore and mudflats of the estuary include Greylag Goose, Whooper Swan, Wigeon, Pintail, Scaup, Pochard, Knot, Bar-tailed Godwit, Greenshank and divers. But interest extends throughout the year with resident breeding terns and waders in summer, and passage migrants in spring and autumn.

□ Access from A9 (north of Inverness) along both shores. Also west of Tain and via B9165 to Tarbat Ness. OS 21: 94 87.

12 Duncansby Head

Lighthouse on head gives fine views of Orkney, the Pentland Skerries and along the east coast. The cliffs and stacks (250 ft/75 m) of Duncansby are interesting geological features which hold important sea bird colonies.

□ East of John O'Groats. Extreme north-east tip of Scotland, off A9. OS 12: 40 73.

13 Dunnet Head

High cliffs (400 ft/120 m) of Old Red Sandstone rise vertically from the sea at Dunnet Head – the most northerly point on the Scottish mainland. Sea bird colonies: Guillemots, Razorbills, Puffins, Kittiwakes, and Fulmars. Cliff-top vegetation with Scottish Primrose and Lovage.

□ Take B855 off A836, 10 miles/16 km north-east of Thurso. OS 12: 20 76.

14 Farigaig Forest Trail

Forestry Commission. Trail through native woodland and forestry plantations to mountain viewpoint overlooking river gorges.

□ (Tel: Inverness 32811). Visitor Centre open Easter–October. 13 miles/20.5 km north-west of Fort Augustus on eastern shore of Loch Ness on B862 then B852. OS 26: 52 23.

15 Glen Affric

Forestry Commission. Classic example of highland glen with mountain, river and loch habitats. Important Caledonian pinewood reserve on south side of glen. Scottish Crossbills in some years. Fishing.

□ Contact Forestry Commission Office at Cannich. Off A831 at Cannich. 25 miles/40 km south-west of Inverness. OS 25: 18 22.

16 Glen Coe

National Trust for Scotland. (Scene of the Massacre of Glen Coe, 1692.) Mountain and moorland habitats for Red Deer, Wild Cat, Ptarmigan, Golden Eagle and flora includes Mossy Saxifrage and Alpine Lady's Mantle. Good climbing and walking country. Visitor Centre.

□ (Tel: Ballachulish 307). 12 miles/19 km south of Fort William on A82. OS 41: 09 58.

17 Glen More Forest Park

Forestry Commission. Plantation of pine and spruce. Mountain, moorland and old Caledonian pinewoods. Fine area for upland animals including Red Deer, Wild Cat, Golden Eagle, Ptarmigan, Capercaillie and the introduced Reindeer. In the centre of the park lies Loch Morlich, 1000 ft/300 m above sea level with sandy beaches surrounded by old pines. Forest trails. Sailing. Fishing.

☐ (Tel: Inverness 32811). Trails open all year. 7 miles/11 km off A9 at Aviemore then by A951 to Loch Morlich. OS 36: 97 09.

18 Glen Tarff

Steep wooded glen at the south of Loch Ness. A mixed deciduous wood of Downy Birch, Sessile Oak, Ash and Wych Elm over a dense shrub layer of Hazel, Bird Cherry and Goat Willow. Woodland plants and birds.

☐ South of Loch Ness, 2 miles/3 km off A82 along A862 for 1 mile/1.6 km then south on minor road to glen. OS 34: 38 07.

19 Great Glen Exhibition

Museum exhibition hall with history of the Great Glen described. Special displays on Loch Ness, its natural history and the legendary Loch Ness Monster.

☐ Open June–September daily (afternoons only on Sunday). In centre of Fort Augustus near Caledonian Canal. OS 34: 37 09.

20 Handa Island

RSPB reserve. Sea bird island with high cliffs (380 ft/120 m). Large number of Guillemots and other sea birds. Inland on the maritime heath, Arctic and Great Skuas, and Red-throated Divers breed.

☐ Island 3 miles/4.5 km north of Scourie. Access by boat from Tarbet off A894 on Scottish mainland. Open April–August (no boats on Sundays). OS 9: 13 48.

21 Highland Wildlife Park

Wildlife Park specializes in highland mammals and birds. Many in natural setting. Drive-through section with Red Deer, Bison and Highland cattle. Also Capercaillie, Ptarmigan, Eagles, Wild Cats, Wolves, Bear and Lynx in enclosures.

☐ (Tel: Kincraig 270). Open March–November. Near Kincraig on A9 south of Aviemore. OS 35: 80 04.

22 Inverewe Garden

National Trust for Scotland. Magnificent garden (over 100 years old) set on sea loch. Exotic plants from Eucalyptus trees to Himalayan lilies and South Pacific giant Forget-me-nots. Fine area for hill and coastal walks. Ranger Service.

☐ (Tel: Poolewe 229). Visitor Centre open April–mid-October. Garden open all year. 6 miles/9.5 km north-east of Gairloch off A832. OS 19: 86 81.

23 Invernaver National Nature Reserve

Nature Conservancy Council. Area of coastal and upland habitats and important botanical sites. It covers dunes, saltmarsh, shingle, cliffs and moorland habitats. A number of northern species including Scottish Primrose and Mountain Milkvetch. An abundance of mountain species growing at low altitudes – Moss Campion, Purple and Yellow Saxifrage and Alpine Bistort. Breeding birds include Red-throated Diver, Common Sandpiper, Greenshank, Twite and Ring Ouzel.

☐ Permit only. Contact Mr W Mackay, 89 Invernaver. Off A836 at Invernaver, 28 miles/44 km west of Thurso. OS 10: 70 60.

24 Inverpolly National Nature Reserve

Nature Conservancy Council. Remote mountain and moorland area. Wide variety of natural habitats:crags, native woodland and mountain summits. Nature and geological trails. Species to be seen include Golden Eagle, Peregrine Falcon, Raven, Pine Marten, Wild Cat and Otter.

☐ (Tel: Elphin 234/Lochinver 204). Information Centre at Knockan Cliff. Open May–September. 11 miles/17.5 km north of Ullapool off A835. OS 15: 18 09.

25 Kintail and Morvich

National Trust for Scotland. Striking West Highland scenery, including Five Sisters of Kintail. Superb walking country. Red Deer and Wild Goats; varied flora. Ranger

Service. Visitor Centre at Morvich Farm.
□(Tel: Balmacara 278). North of A87 to
Kyle of Lochalsh. OS 33: 95 21.

26 Knockfin Heights
Large area of upland bogs on a plateau
1416 ft/431 m high. Plants and animals
typical of undisturbed peatland. See also
Caithness Flows.
□East of A897, 5 miles/8 km south of For-
sinard Hotel and railway station. South of
Melvich. OS 17: 91 34.

27 Landmark Visitor Centre
Interpretative Centre using audio-visual
techniques to demonstrate Highland his-
tory. Nature trail. Woodland walk.
□(Tel: Carrbridge 613). Open all year. In
Carrbridge on A9. North of Aviemore.
OS 36: 90 22.

28 Loch-an-Eilein
Nature Conservancy Council. Loch is in
Scots Pine woodland. Species include
Roe Deer, Red Squirrel and many smaller
animals; Treecreepers and Scottish
Crossbill. In loch-side meadows abundant
butterflies and dragonflies in summer. Vis-
itor Centre has exhibits on history of native
Scots Pine forests.
□Visitor Centre open May–September. 2½
miles/4 km south of Aviemore off B970.
OS 36: 89 08.

29 Loch Fleet
Scottish Wildlife Trust. Tidal basin of Loch
Fleet attracts numbers of wintering wildfowl including Mallard, Teal, Wigeon,
Goldeneye, Eider, Red-breasted Merganser and Shelduck whilst the outer shore
between Embo and Golspie often has
large rafts of Common and Velvet Scoters
or Long-tailed Duck. Inland of Loch Fleet
and separated by an embankment (The
Mound) carrying the A9 and disused railway line lies an area of freshwater marsh
and woodland of Alder, Willow and Birch.
This area (Mound Alderwoods National
Nature Reserve/Nature Conservancy
Council) is rich in breeding birds and has
an unusual pattern of plant communities.
□Nature reserve access is restricted but
reserve may be viewed from public roads.

4 miles/6.5 km north of Dornorch. East of
A9 on minor road which follows south
shore of loch.

30 Loch Garten
RSPB reserve famous for Ospreys since
their return in 1959. Surrounding area has
a variety of rich wildlife habitats including
Caledonian pine forests and moorland
with Crossbill, Crested Tit, Capercaillie,
Red Squirrel and Deer.
□Access into bird sanctuary around
Osprey breeding site strictly forbidden.
(Tel: Boat of Garten 648). 8 miles/12.5 km
north-east of Aviemore. Off B970 along
signposted track to RSPB Osprey Observation Post. OS 36: 97 18.

31 Loch Insh and Insh Marshes
Part RSPB reserve. Whole area is about
2470 acres/1000 ha of marshland and
bogs rich in wetland birds and plants.
Great variety of breeding and over-
wintering duck and waders. Wetlands also
important staging post for migrating birds
in spring and autumn.
□Reserve open April–August on Wednesday, Friday and Sunday. Between B970
and A9 from Kingussie to Kincraig. 12
miles/19 km south-west of Aviemore.
OS 35: 77 99.

32 Loch Maree Woods
Area of great interest to those wishing to
study the wildlife of native Scottish
forests. The woods of Glas Leitire on the
south shore of the loch and the lower
slopes of Beinn Eighe to 960 ft/300 m are
native pinewoods with variable cover.
Although much modified by man, they still
contain fine examples of pinewood plant
communities, especially the tall Heather,
Bilberry, Cowberry; these grow over dense
mosses and other rare pinewood plants.
Rich animal life including Wild Cat and
Pine Marten, Buzzard and Sparrowhawk.
North of the loch are Sessile Oak with Ash,
Hazel, Birch, Alder and some Pine and an
interesting ground flora. Nature trails. See
also Beinn Eighe National Nature Reserve.
□From Kinlochewe take A832, 3 miles/
4.5 km north-west to Glas Leitire or to north
shore of loch. OS 19: 00 64.

33 Rock Wood Ponds

Forestry Commission. Circular trail around small lochans. Interpretation boards on bird life. Waterfowl. Cliff paths with good views of Cairngorms. Picnic places.
☐ (Tel: Kincraig 223). 6 miles/9.5 km south of Aviemore off B970 for Inshriach Forest. OS 35 or 36: 83 02.

34 Speyside Woods

The B970 follows the Spey valley and passes two of the largest and finest examples of native pinewoods in Britain. One follows the Spey valley between Loch-an-Eilein turning off the B970 to Loch Insh. The other is Abernethy Forest (which includes Loch Garten) and is accessible off the B970 along the minor road signposted to Loch Garten. South of Nethybridge on B970, east of Carrbridge, a circular road via Aundorach will give botanists and bird-watchers a variety of habitats to explore. Twinflower and Wintergreen are amongst the special pinewood plants. Also Scotch Argus butterfly, Wild Cat, Badger, Red Deer, Red Squirrel, Golden Eagle, Buzzard, Sparrowhawk, Capercaillie, Siskin, Crested Tit, Black Grouse and Crossbill. See also Cairngorm Mountains, part National Nature Reserve and Loch Garten.
☐ Off B970 at Aviemore, the woods lie north and south. OS 36: 89 11.

35 Strontian Glen Nature Trail

Nature Conservancy Council. Nature trail covering woodland, riverine, moorland and mountain habitat. Upland flora and fauna. See Arriundle Oakwood National Nature Reserve.
☐ (Tel: Inverness 39431). 2 miles/3 km north of Strontian, off A861. South-west of Fort William. OS 40: 82 63.·

36 Torridon

National Trust for Scotland. Mountain habitats (3000 ft/900 m) of geological and botanical interest.
☐ Visitor Centre and Deer Museum at road junction to Diabeg. Open June–September. (Tel: Torridon 221). 8 miles/12.5 km south-west of Kinlochewe, off A896. Road runs along Glen Torridon. OS 24: 89 56.

Islands

Orkney, Shetland and the Western Isles, best known for their bird life, are also very interesting botanically. Mountain plants grow at unusually low altitudes on these exposed islands. The machair (see page 23) on the Western Isles is especially rich in flora. The special "maritime" climate experienced in the islands means that unusual species grow on the marshes, bogs and moorlands.

The islands are famous for their spectacular sea bird colonies: these boast some of the highest numbers and the greatest concentrations in Britain. There is also a large breeding wildfowl and wader population, supplemented by over-wintering species from the Arctic. The islands are also amongst the best areas for observing Scotland's birds of prey.

On the **Orkney Islands**, sea bird colonies include Kittiwake, Guillemot, Black Guillemot, Razorbill, Fulmar, Cormorant, Shag and Puffin. Raven and Peregrine breed on cliffs whilst inland, Hen Harrier, Great Skua breed. Nesting wildfowl and breeders include Red-necked Phalarope, Eider, Red-breasted Merganser, Tufted Duck. In winter Whooper and Mute Swans, Scaup, Long-tailed Duck, Pochard and Tufted Duck visit the islands.

On **Shetland**, the main sea bird colonies are similar to those on the Orkney Islands with Manx Shearwater, Storm Petrel, and Gannet. Other breeding birds include Eider, Twite, Skua, Tern, Red-necked Phalarope, Whimbrel, Raven, Merlin, Peregrine, Red-throated Diver, Red-breasted Merganser, and Corncrake. In winter, Great Northern Diver, Scoter, Long-tailed Duck, Eider, Red-breasted Merganser, Glaucous and Iceland Gulls are regular visitors.

On the **Western Isles**, mountains and moorlands are valuable breeding habitats for Golden Eagle, Hen Harrier, Buzzard, Merlin, Short-eared Owl and Raven. Sea bird colonies similar to the Orkney Islands also include Leach's Petrel, Storm Petrel and Manx Shearwater. A variety of wildfowl and waders breed on shore and loch side – Greylag Geese, Little Grebe, Eider, Shelduck, Wigeon, Shoveler, Teal, Gadwall, Oystercatcher, Ringed Plover, Redshank and Red-necked Phalarope. Inland, Great Skua, Arctic Skua, Golden Plover and Greenshank breed. In winter these islands are excellent for watching sea duck, geese, waders and divers.

ORKNEY
37 Copinsay
RSPB reserve. Sea bird colonies. Interesting coastal vegetation.
☐ Island off Mainland Orkney. By boat from Newark Bay. (Tel: Deerness 245). OS 6: 610 010.

38 Loch of Stenness and Loch of Harray
Good for watching wildfowl in winter. Sea duck found on brackish Stennes and freshwater duck on Harray. Breeding ducks and waders.
☐ North-east of Stromness. Take A965 and at Waith Bridge turn left onto B9055 which runs between the lochs. On Mainland Orkney. OS 6: 30 12.

39 Mainland Orkney
Three RSPB reserves on the mainland. Two of them are moorlands: Dale of Cottasgarth and Hobbister are good for watching birds of prey such as Hen Harrier and Skua. The third is at Marwick Head, good for cliff-nesting sea birds.
☐ Access unrestricted. On Mainland Orkney. OS 6.

40 North Hill
RSPB reserve famous for large colony of Arctic Terns.
☐ Contact the Warden, c/o Gowrie, Papa Westray, Orkney. Access best between mid-May–July. Ferry from Kirkwall on Mainland Orkney. OS 5: 496 538.

41 Noup Cliffs
RSPB reserve. Cliff-nesting sea bird colonies. Largest colony of Guillemots in Britain. Cliff-top vegetation.
☐ On Westray. Off road to Noup Head lighthouse (please close gates). Ferry

from Kirkwall on Mainland Orkney. OS 5: 392 500.

42 Old Man of Hoy
A stack rising 440 ft/138 m from the sea. Sea bird colonies. Also Peregrine Falcon. Rich flora on Cuilags and Ward Hills on Hoy. Upland heaths include Reindeer Moss and mountain species at low altitude. Best example of native woodlands in the Orkneys at Berriedale with Downy Birch, Willow, Aspen and Rowan.
☐ North-west of island of Hoy for stack. Ferry from Stromness on Mainland Orkney to Lyness on Hoy. OS 7: 17 00.

SHETLAND
43 Fair Isle
National Trust for Scotland. Internationally famous Bird Observatory on notable migration route. Sea bird colonies. Eider ducks.
☐ Observatory open March–November. Island midway between Orkney and Shetland. Access by mailboat (twice weekly). OS 4: inset.

44 Fetlar
Part RSPB reserve. Former nesting site of Snowy Owls still to be seen. Sea bird colonies also noted for waders. Good flora; area has a type of grassheath known as serpentine.
☐ Island access by boat from Lerwick on Mainland Shetland. Reserve May–July and by arrangement with the Warden, Bealance, Bothy, Fetlar, Shetland. OS 1: 603 917.

45 Hermaness National Nature Reserve
Nature Conservancy Council. Sea bird colonies on cliffs. Grey Seals.
☐ Northern tip of Unst. Ferries connect Unst and Yell, Yell and Mainland Shetland. OS 1: 60 18.

46 Lerwick
Good touring centre. Scalloway coast to west has over-wintering Glaucous and Iceland Gulls and Long-tailed Duck. Loch of Clickimin off A970 good for wintering duck and waders. Shetland Museum.
☐ On Mainland Shetland. OS 4: 47 41.

47 Mousa
Famous for its prehistoric stone tower (broch) in which Storm Petrels nest. Good for sea birds and Eider ducks. Seals.
☐ Island off Sandwick, south of Lerwick on Mainland Shetland. Boat to island May–September (afternoons only). OS 4: 45 24.

48 Noss National Nature Reserve
Nature Conservancy Council/RSPB. Fine sea bird colonies. Eider congregate off the Noup of Noss in spring. Cliff flowers.
☐ Access from Lerwick to Bressay and then via Noss Sound Ferry to Noss. OS 4: 53 41.

49 Ronas Hill and North Roe
Area of diverse habitats: sea cliffs, moorland, bogs and the highest ground (1440 ft/450 m) in the Shetland Islands. Interesting vegetation particularly alpine species on Ronas Hill, scrub around lochs and unusual peat mounds on North Roe supporting heathers. Breeding sites of Great Skuas. Large Grey Seal population.
☐ 3 miles/4.5 km west of Collafirth on A970 north of Lerwick on Mainland Shetland. OS 3: 30 83.

50 Scousburgh
Good touring centre, close to Loch of Spiggie with wintering wildfowl. Sea bird colonies on nearby cliffs and south on Sunburgh Head. Shetland plant specialities on moorland and marsh habitats.
☐ South of Lerwick on Mainland Shetland. OS 4: 37 17.

WESTERN ISLES
51 Balranald
RSPB reserve. Area of great importance for breeding divers, ducks, waders, Corncrake and Tern. Also wildfowl. Diverse habitats: machair, freshwater lochs and marshland with important plant communities.
☐ On North Uist. Contact the Warden, Goular, Hougharry, Lochmaddy, North Uist before visiting. Ferry from Isle of Harris or Uig on Isle of Skye. OS 18: 707 707.

52 Butt of Lewis
Good point for watching sea birds on migration and sea bird colonies. Also Loch Stiapavat on peninsula for breeding and wintering wildfowl including Spotted Crake and sandflats to south-east at Port of Ness to Skigersta for sea ducks.
☐ Northern tip of Isle of Lewis. Ferry from Ullapool to Stornoway on Lewis. OS 8: 51 66.

53 Griminish Point
Sea bird colonies. Golden Eagle, Raven, Golden Plover, Greenshank, Arctic Skua and Corncrake breed inland.
☐ On North Uist. Headland on north-west coast. Ferry to Lochmaddy on Uist from Uig on Isle of Skye. OS 18: 725 766.

54 Grogarry
Coastal lochs, lagoons and machair. Rich in plants and birds, especially breeding waders and ducks (also Black-throated Diver).
☐ On South Uist, north of Lochboisdale. Ferry from Oban or from North Uist via Benbecuela. OS 22: 77 39.

55 Loch Druidibeg
National Nature Reserve
Nature Conservancy Council. Breeding Greylag Geese, waders, ducks. Machair near loch is botanically rich.
☐ On South Uist. Contact the Warden, Kinloch, Grogarry, South Uist. (Tel: Grogarry 252). Ferry from Oban. OS 22: 77 39.

56 Lochmaddy
Good for over-wintering geese and ducks. Offshore islands of Berneray, Pabbay, Ensay, Coppay and Shillay are all of some interest.
☐ East coast of North Uist. Ferry from Tarbert on Isle of Harris or Uig on Isle of Skye. OS 18: 91 68.

57 Rhum National Nature Reserve
National Trust for Scotland/Nature Conservancy Council. Coastal habitats with interesting plant communities. Sea bird colonies. Inland is a large colony of Manx Shearwaters. Golden Eagle seen on coast and mountain cliffs. Inland area mostly mountains and moorland with Peregrine Falcon, Raven, Red-throated Divers, Corncrakes and upland waders.

☐Isle of Rhum. Contact Chief Warden, Nature Conservancy Council, White House, Kinloch, Isle of Rhum. (Tel: Rhum 26). Open all year. Ferry from Mallaig and Arisaig on mainland Scotland. OS 39: 40 99.

58 St Kilda
National Nature Reserve
Island group. National Trust for Scotland/ Nature Conservancy Council. Sea bird colonies. On Boreray and its stacks is the world's largest Gannetry (over 100,000 birds). St Kilda has its own distinct species of wren, mouse and sheep (Soay Sheep). Grey Seals. Unusual flora.
☐Access by excursions and working parties organized by National Trust for Scotland (see page 123). OS 18: inset.

59 Stornaway
Good base for touring Lewis. Woodlands in Lewis Castle noted for bird life. Harbour has wintering duck and Iceland and Glaucous Gulls. Loch Branahuie on eastern edge of town also good for wintering duck. North-east of town Melbost Sands have wildfowl and waders including Common and Velvet Scoters, and Purple Sandpiper. Popular sea-angling resort.
☐Isle of Lewis. Stornoway reached by ferry from Ullapool or Uig on Isle of Skye via Tarbert. OS 8: 42 32.

Grampian

60 Balmoral Castle and Woodlands
Speyside remnants of ancient Caledonian pine forests in grounds of Balmoral Castle. Nearby at Ballochbuie Forest is another area of Scots Pine woodland. Crossbill, Capercaillie and woodland plants typical of native pine forests.
☐Castle open May–July (except Sundays and when Royal Family are in residence). At Balmoral on A93, 8 miles/12.5 km west of Ballater. OS 44: 25 94.

61 Buchan Cliffs
Sea bird colonies. Cliff-top vegetation with Juniper, Spring Squill, Lovage, Stone Bramble and Roseroot.

☐Area extends from Boddam to Collieston including the spectacular Bullers of Bucham chasm. 10 miles/16 km of sea cliffs and sandy bay (Cruden Bay). 7 miles/11 km south of Peterhead on A952 then B9108. OS 30: 13 42.

62 Crathes Castle Estate
National Trust for Scotland. Grounds have eight gardens with great Yew hedges over 250 years old. Woodland nature trails. Visitor Centre. Ranger Service.
☐(Tel: Crathes 651). Castle open May– September (daily and afternoons on Sundays). Gardens and grounds open all year. 3 miles/4.5 km east of Banchory off A93. OS 45: 73 96.

63 Crawton Cliffs
Sea bird colonies on low cliffs with good access and easy viewing.
☐3 miles/4.5 km south of Stonehaven off A92 to Crawton. Then walk northwards. OS 45: 87 79.

64 Culbin Forest and Coast
Forestry Commission/RSPB. Large area of coast and woodland habitats noted for its bird life. Freshwater lochs (Loch Loy and Cran Loch). Pinewoods contain Crested Tit, Crossbill and Capercaillie. On the coast and in the Findhorn estuary are large numbers of over-wintering waders and wildfowl. Wigeon, Common Scoter, Red-breasted Merganser, Tufted Duck, Goldeneye and Long-tailed Duck. Vast sand dune system, once the largest in Britain. Many plant species reach their northern limits on the east coast at this site. Acid dunes and slacks with associated plant communities. Small tern colony (offshore sand bars part RSPB).
☐Off A96, 3 miles/4.5 km east of Forres to Findhorn village. OS 27: 04 64.

65 Drum Castle Estate
National Trust for Scotland. Old Forest of Drum. Mixed woodland of Birch, Oak and Pine. Woodland walks. Ranger Service.
☐(Tel: Crathes 651). Castle open May– September. Grounds open all year. 10 miles/16 km south-west of Aberdeen off A93. OS 38: 79 00.

66 Falconer Museum

Museum with natural history exhibits including fossils.
☐ Off Main Street, Forres on A96. Open May–September. OS 27: 03 58.

67 Findhorn Bay

Fine areas of saltmarsh vegetation and extensive mudflats noted for waders and ducks in winter. Sand dune system (with interesting flora) east of Findhorn. Exceptionally rich birdwatching area with sea duck, waders and geese; noted for migrant waders.
☐ Between Forres and Findhorn off A96. At Forres several minor roads lead from B9011 to the bay. OS 27: 04 64.

68 Glen Muick and Lochnagar

Scottish Wildlife Trust. Mountain area with alpine flora on summit plateau. Suitable for well-prepared hill walkers. Lochnagar possesses a superb corrie with cliffs cut deeply by ravines. Ranger Service.
☐ Leave A93 at Ballater to Glen Muick trail from The Hut marked on OS map to summit. 3 miles/4.5 km. OS 44: 30 85.

69 Glen Tanar

Large area of native pinewood (4940 acres/2000 ha) – part of the once extensive Speyside woodlands. See also Balmoral Castle. Birds and plants include Crossbill, Capercaillie, Wintergreen and Twinflower.
☐ 15 miles/24 km south-west of Banchory off A93. OS 37 or 44: 47 95.

70 Hazlehead Nature Trails

Nature trails through parkland and woodland. Many interesting plants and small mammals.
☐ Hazlehead Park, off Queen's Road on western outskirts of Aberdeen off A944. (Tel: Aberdeen 23456). Open all year.

71 Leith Hall Estate

National Trust for Scotland. Grounds include rock garden, two ponds, bird observation hide and countryside walks. Soay Sheep. Ranger Service.
☐ (Tel: Crathes 651). Leith Hall open daily May–September (afternoons on Sundays).

Gardens and grounds open all year. 7 miles/11 km south of Huntly on A97 then B9002. OS 37: 53 29.

72 Loch of Skene

Wintering duck congregate on this small loch in great numbers. Noted for large flocks of Wigeon in autumn.
☐ View from road or contact Aberdeen–Stonehaven Yacht Club, Portlethen, Aberdeenshire for access. (Tel: Aberdeen 780748). 10 miles/16 km west of Aberdeen off A944. OS 38: 78 08.

73 Loch of Strathbeg

RSPB reserve. Wetland area close to the coast with breeding waterfowl and over-wintering geese and duck. Pink-footed and Greylag Geese, Mute and Whooper Swans, Pochard, Tufted Duck, Wigeon, Goosander and Goldeneye. In summer Eider and Shelduck breed on sand dunes between loch and sea. Interesting flora on dunes. Dune species, saltmarsh and freshwater plant communities at the northern end of loch. Sea Milkwort near sea and various orchids in marshy areas.
☐ By advance arrangement only. Contact the Warden, The Lythe, Crimmonmogate, Lonmay, Fraserburgh AB4 4UB. Open all year. On A952, 10 miles/16 km south-east of Fraserburgh. OS 30: 07 59.

74 Macduff Cliffs–Pennan Head

Area of coastal cliffs and bays with rich cliff vegetation. Pennan Head and Troup Head best for sea bird colonies. Geological interest. Dangerous cliffs: keep away from edges.
☐ From Macduff eastwards 9 miles/14.5 km west of Fraserburgh off B9031 at Pennan. OS 29: 71 64.

75 Mar Forest

Moorland (area of ancient Caledonian pine forests) with special plants, deer, Red Squirrels and woodland birds including Crossbill and Capercaillie. The once extensive pinewoods now confined to small areas at Glens Lui Beg, Derry and Quoich are fine examples of a nationally rare habitat.
☐ 7 miles/11 km west of Braemar off A93

along minor road to Glen Lui then north to Derry Lodge. OS 43: 08 89.

76 Muir of Dinnet
National Nature Reserve
Nature Conservancy Council. Areas of diverse habitats including moorland, marshland, Birchwood and lochs. Water-fowl population, both breeding and over-wintering, are main interest.
□(Tel: Dinnet 369) Nature trail open all year. 3 miles/4.5 km east of Ballater off A93 or west of Aboyne. OS 37 or 44: 45 98.

77 Peterhead Bay
Noted for over-wintering congregations of sea duck along with waders in sheltered harbour. Viewing at close quarters often possible throughout the winter. Divers, Red-breasted Merganser, Eider.
□On south side of Peterhead off A952. OS 30: 12 45.

78 Pitmedden Estate
National Trust for Scotland. Formal gar-den. Woodland and farmland walk. Rare breeds of livestock. Ranger Service.
□(Tel: Crathes 651). On edge of Pitmed-den. Open all year. 13 miles/20.5 km north-west of Aberdeen on A92 then B999. OS 38: 88 27.

79 St Cyrus National Nature Reserve
Nature Conservancy Council. Rich botan-ical area of coastal flats, sand dunes, cliffs and pasture. Lime-rich sand dune past-ures possess some of the best examples of dune vegetation. Uncommon species and some at their northern limit in Britain, such as Nottingham Catchfly, Clustered Bellflower, Rough Clover, Wild Liquorice, Purple Milk-vetch and Maiden Pink.
□Permit only. Contact Nature Conser-vancy Council Regional Office, 17 Rubis-law Terrace, Aberdeen. (Tel: Aberdeen 572863). 5 miles/8 km north-east of Mon-trose off A92. OS 45: 75 64.

80 Sands of Forvie and Ythan Estuary
National Nature Reserve
Nature Conservancy Council. Sands of Forvie famous for breeding colony of Eiders — the largest in Britain (2000 pairs).

Sandwich, Common, Arctic and Little Terns and Shelduck also breed. Ythan Estuary good for watching wintering wild-fowl and waders. Pink-footed and Greylag Geese, Whooper Swan, Eider, Wigeon, Mallard, Shelduck, Goldeneye, Pochard, Redshank, Bar-tailed and Black-tailed Godwits, Whimbrel, Green Sandpiper, Ruff, Spotted Redshank on migration.
□Permit only. Contact Nature Conser-vancy Council Regional Office, 17 Rubis-law Terrace, Aberdeen. (Tel: Aberdeen 572863). 13 miles/20 km north of Aber-deen off A92 then the A975 to Newburgh follows estuary. Nature reserve access via Collieston on B9003. OS 38: 99 25.

81 Spey Estuary
Speymouth is an interesting variety of channels, sand bars and island with coastal and scrub plant communities. Kingston on the estuary provides good views of the area. Rich in bird life including sea ducks, terns, waders and sea birds. Species include Wigeon, Teal, Red-breasted Merganser, Goldeneye, Velvet and Common Scoters, Turnstone, Bar-tailed Godwit, Whimbrel, Green-shank, Cormorant.
□8 miles/12.5 km north-east of Elgin off A96 along B9015 to Kingston. OS 28: 34 65.

Tayside

82 Arbroath Cliffs Nature Trail
Scottish Wildlife Trust. Cliff-top nature trail with varied flora and fauna.
□Trail starts from the Esplanade, Arbroath on A92. (Tel: Forfar 62517). OS 54: 64 40.

83 Ben Lawers
National Nature Reserve
National Trust for Scotland/Nature Con-servancy Council. High mountain (3984 ft/1200 m) and moorland habitats. Famous for arctic-alpine flora. Upland birds. Visitor Centre with historical and geological displays. Nature trail. Guided walks (summer only).
□(Tel: Killin 397/248). 4 miles/6.5 km north-east of Killin on A827. OS 51: 67 39.

84 Black Wood of Rannoch

Forestry Commission. The woodlands around Loch Rannoch are amongst the largest areas of native pinewood remaining in Scotland. South of the loch, Scots Pine and Birch dominate and to the north there are Oaks. The whole of the Tummel valley (Strath Tummel) is of interest and can be viewed from B846. The area is known for its insects, plants and birds, which include Capercaillie, Black Grouse, Scottish Crossbill, Redpoll and Woodcock. Numerous duck species may be found in the lochs in winter. Forest walks. Fishing. See also Rannoch Moor.
□20 miles/32 km west of Pitlochry along B8019, then B846 turning south at Kinloch Rannoch for minor road to south bank of Loch Rannoch. OS 42 or 51: 61 57.

85 Camperdown Park

Nature trail through parkland, plantation, woodland, wildfowl pond. Nature Centre. Ranger Service.
□(Tel: Dundee 645444). 4 miles/6.5 km north-west of Dundee off A923 at junction with A972. OS 54: 36 32.

86 Glenshee Chairlift

The area round the chairlift consists of limestone uplands of special interest to botanists for its arctic-alpine flora. Rich area for mountain species.
□12 miles/19 km south of Braemar off A93. OS 43: 14 76.

87 The Hermitage

National Trust for Scotland. Woodland walks by the Hermitage – an eighteenth-century folly above a gorge. Douglas Fir and Scots Pine. Ranger Service.
□(Tel: Killiecrankie 233). 2 miles/3 km west of Dunkeld off B898. OS 58: 00 41.

88 Linn of Tummel

National Trust for Scotland. Nature trails along wooded valleys of Garry and Tummel. Ranger Service. Talks and film shows.
□Information Centre at Killiecrankie. (Tel: Killiecrankie 233). 3 miles/4.5 km north of Pitlochry on A9 then B8079. Open March–September. OS 43: 91 61.

89 Loch of Drumellie

Often large numbers of over-wintering duck and geese. Greylag Geese, Whooper Swan, Wigeon, Pochard, Shoveler,Tufted Duck, Goldeneye and Goosander.
□2½ miles/4 km west of Blairgowire off A923. 2 miles/3 km farther west is Loch Clunie which can also be viewed from A923. OS 53: 14 44.

90 Loch of the Lowes Reserve

Scottish Wildlife Trust. Nesting waterbirds including Ospreys may be watched from hides. Visitor Centre with exhibition on ecology of the area. Ranger Service.
□(Tel: Dunkeld 337/Ballinluig 267). 2 miles/3 km east of Dunkeld off A923. OS 53: 04 43.

91 Montrose Basin

Scottish Wildlife Trust. Large numbers of wildfowl and waders feed and roost in autumn and winter. Waders (up to 20,000) include Knot, Oystercatcher, Dunlin, Bar-tailed Godwit and Ringed Plover. Noted for its autumn roost of nearly 10,000 terns (Common, Sandwich and Arctic). Salt-marsh flora on western shore. Ranger Service.
□Contact Scottish Wildlife Trust (see page 123). South of A935 west of Montrose. OS 54: 71 57.

92 Pitlochry Power Station and Dam

Famous for its "fish ladder" where Salmon can be observed through windows climbing from River Tummel to Loch Faskally, which was created by the dam.
□(Tel: Pitlochry 2271). Open Easter–September. Off A9 in Pitlochry. OS 52: 94 58.

93 Rannoch Moor,
part National Nature Reserve

Part Nature Conservancy Council. Large area of blanket bog, moorland and lochans in a depression at over 1000 ft/300 m altitude. A range of bog plants and insects of scientific importance. See also Black Wood of Rannoch.
□Access via Rannoch railway station at end of B846 (which joins B8019 then A9 at Pitlochry). OS 51: 42 57.

94 Tay Estuary
North bank of the Tay estuary has fine reed-fringed marshes leading to extensive intertidal mudflats. The whole area is of national importance for feeding and roosting geese, duck and waders in winter. In autumn large flocks of up to 20,000 Pinkfooted Geese congregate before moving to wintering grounds.
☐West of Dundee (north bank) access at Kingoodie and Port Allen, all off B958. OS 59: 33 29/25 21. Or at Newburgh off A913 on south bank. OS 58: 23 18.

95 Tummel Forest Centre
Forestry Commission. Interpretation Centre. Walks mainly through various ages of conifer plantations.
☐(Tel: Killiecrankie 223). Centre open April–September. Trails open all year and start off A9 north of Pitlochry. OS 43: 85 60.

96 Vane Farm
RSPB reserve covering Loch Leven area with wetland, moorland and woodland habitats. Important wildfowl site. Overwintering geese (Pink-footed and Greylag) and ducks. Large population of breeding ducks. Visitor Centre.
☐(Tel: Kinross 62355). Open April–October (except Friday), November–March (weekends only). South end of Loch Leven, 4 miles/6.5 km south of Kinross on B9097. Leave M90 at junction 5 or 6 from Perth. OS 58: 16 99.

Strathclyde

97 Aber Bogs
A mixture of swamp, scrubland and open pools. Wetland plants and bird life.
☐The area is in the southern part of the Loch Lomond marshes where the River Endrick joins the loch. 10 miles/16 km north of Glasgow on A811. OS 56: 43 88.

98 Ailsa Craig
Private island. Sea bird colonies with large Gannetry. Geological interest.
Small island in Firth of Clyde. Boat from Girvan: weekdays in summer only. (Tel: Girvan 2631). OS 76: 02 99.

99 Ardmore
Scottish Wildlife Trust. Promontory on north side of Clyde estuary. Wide range of habitats. Part of Ardmore is a Site of Special Scientific Interest. Ducks and waders and coastal plants.
☐Promontory 3 miles/4.5 km south-east of Helensburgh, north-west of Glasgow on A814. OS 63: 319 786.

100 Argyll Forest Park
Forestry Commission. Vast area of the West Highlands with rugged uplands and sea lochs. Forest walks, several with wildlife interest. Picnic places. Sea angling.
☐Contact Ardgartan Forestry Commission 3 miles/4.5 km west of Arrochar on A83. Forest Park approach via A82 from Loch Lomond, A83 from Inveraray, A815 from Strachur or south from Dunoon. OS 56: 29 04.

101 Botanic Gardens
Gardens include Victorian greenhouses, one with famous fernery, glasshouses with orchids and palms.
☐Great Western Road, off A82, Glasgow. Open all year.

102 Brodick Castle and Country Park
Isle of Arran. National Trust for Scotland. Rhododendron garden and pleasant woodland walks. Park includes Goatfell (2866 ft/870 m) the highest peak on Arran, offering good hillwalks and a variety of mountain wildlife including Red Deer. Ranger Service.
☐(Tel: Brodick 2202). Gardens and Country Park open all year. Castle open Easter Sunday and 18–30th April, Monday, Wednesday and Saturday afternoons only. May–September daily and Sunday afternoons. Ferry via Ardrossan 25 miles/40 km south-west of Glasgow off A78. Castle and park 1½ miles/2 km north of Brodick pier. OS 69: 01 37.

103 Calderpark Zoo
Zoo with small collection of mammals, reptiles and birds. Undergoing expansion.
☐At Uddingston. (Tel; Glasgow 771 1185). Open all year. 6 miles/9.5 km east of Glasgow city centre off A74.

104 Cameron Park

Wildlife Park and gardens, country house, leisure activities.

☐Open Easter–September. North of Balloch, off A82 at Loch Lomond. OS 56: 37 82.

105 Clachan Bridge

Bridge across "Atlantic Ocean" over Seil Sound which has one of the finest collections of intertidal flora and fauna.

☐Turn off A816 at Kilninver on B884, 10 miles/16 km south-west of Oban. OS 55: 78 19.

106 Colonsay

Island with rich mixture of woodland, moorland, coastal cliffs and dunes providing a wealth of botanical and ornithological interests. Winter birds include Greylag and sometimes Barnacle Geese from neighbouring Oronsay and Mallard, Teal, Wigeon and Tufted Duck. Sea bird colonies; breeding terns. Most of the coastline is of interest.

☐Island 8 miles/12.5 km west of Jura. Ferry from Oban. OS 61.

107 Crarae Woodland Garden

Rhododendrons, Azaleas, trees and shrubs, in a steep glen beside Loch Fyne.

☐ Open March–October. 12 miles/19 km north-east of Lochgilphead. OS 55: 99 97.

108 Culzean Castle and Country Park

National Trust for Scotland. The first Country Park in Scotland. Grounds include orangery, aviary, woodland and swan pond. The castle is perched on a cliff and the coastal edge of the park is good for sea birds and cliff flora. Interpretation Centre. Guided walks. Ranger Service.

☐Open all year. Off A719, 12 miles/19 km south of Ayr. OS 70: 23 09.

109 Enterkine Wood

Scottish Wildlife Trust. Nature reserve. Mixed valley woodland, stream. Red Squirrel, Badger, woodland flora.

☐Permit only. Contact the Warden, 38 Leven Road, Troon, Ayrshire. (Tel: Troon 313 939). 7 miles/11 km north-east of Ayr on A758 then B742. OS 70: 42 23.

110 Falls of Clyde Reserve

Scottish Wildlife Trust. Nature reserve in deep wooded gorge of the River Clyde. Woodland flora and fauna. Nature trail on Corehouse side. Ranger Service.

☐(Tel: Lanark 61345). Corehouse side 1 mile/1.6 km south of Kirkfieldbank, near Lanark. East bank south of New Lanark, south-east of Glasgow off A73. OS 72: 88 41.

111 Finlaystone

Country estate. Woodland walks, formal gardens. Ranger Service (summer only).

☐(Tel: Langbank 285/235). Open all year. Off A8, 5 miles/8 km east of Greenock. OS 63: 36 73.

112 Glendaruel

Forestry Commission. Wildlife observation hides. Forest walks. Picnic places.

☐Contact Forestry Commission, Hafton, Tighnabruaich. (Tel: Tighnabruaich 284). Open all year. 5 miles/8 km north of Tighnabruaich off A8003. OS 63: 00 80.

113 Glen Nant National Nature Reserve

Forestry Commission/Nature Conservancy Council. A steep wooded glen providing a scenic drive to the north shore of Loch Awe and Inverliever Forest. Glen Nant is a fine example of coppiced mixed deciduous woodland. Rich ground flora with Globeflower, Primrose, Birdsnest Orchid, Mountain Melick, ferns. Forest trail.

☐Alongside B845 (off A85) south of Taynuilt 12 miles/19 km west of Oban. OS 50: 01 30.

114 Inverliever Forest Trails

Forestry Commission. Walks through old woodland and mature conifers, passing Badger setts.

☐Contact Forestry Commission, 21 Dalavich Taynuilt, Argyll. (Tel: Loch Avich 258). Trail open all year. North-west of Lochgilphead on A816 then B840 and at Ford along minor road on western shore of Loch Awe. OS 55: 96 11.

115 Islay and Jura

Two islands offering an exceptionally wide range of wildlife habitats including a varied coastline with cliffs, dunes, saltmarsh and shingle, moorland, woodland. The sea lochs, Loch Grunart and Loch Indall, are particularly good for bird life. Winter bird life includes Barnacle Geese, Greenland White-fronted Geese and Great Northern Diver, Scaup, Eider, Wigeon. In summer breeding birds include Red-breasted Merganser, Eider, auks, Kittiwake, Buzzard, Golden Eagle and Chough. Complex of rich habitats provides good variety of flora and insect life.

☐ Ferry from Tarbert on A83 in North Kintyre. Islay: OS 60; Jura: OS 61.

116 Kelburn Country Centre

Countryside Interpretation Centre with nature trails and exhibitions, gardens, leisure activities.

☐ (Tel: Fairlie 685). 2 miles/3 km south of Largs at Fairlie, off A78. OS 63: 208 550.

117 Knapdale

Forestry Commission. Walks through woodland hill and loch scenery. Rich in wildlife. Fishing in six hill lochs.

☐ Contact Forestry Commission, Cairnbaan, Lochgilphead, Argyll. (Tel: Lochgilphead 2304). 5 miles/8 km from Lochgilphead on A816 then B841. OS 55: 82 90.

118 Linn Park Nature Centre

Woodland trails by river, varied plant and animal life. Highland cattle.

☐ Carmunock Road, Glasgow. (Tel: Glasgow 552 7941). Open all year. South of city centre past Rutherglen off A727.

119 Loch Lomond
National Nature Reserve

Nature Conservancy Council. Mainland portion is a wintering ground for wildfowl. Wooded island of Inchcailloch has rich flora and nature trail.

☐ (Tel: Drymen 428). Nature reserve situated south-east of loch. A814 and A82 access from Glasgow to Balloch. Then east along A811 to Gartocharn for Mainland and Drymen and north along B837 to Balmaha for Inchcailloch. Boat from Balmaha Boatyard. (Tel: Balmaha 214). OS 56: 42 91.

120 Lochwinnoch

RSPB reserve. Water marshland and woodland habitats with range of bird life which can be observed from hides near the loch. Nature Centre with viewing tower, exhibition, information.

☐ (Tel: Lochwinnoch 842 663). At Lochwinnoch village off A760. 10 miles/16 km east of Largs. OS 63: 35 58.

121 Lunga Wildlife Reserve

Mixed habitat reserve, moorland, woodland, farmland. Captive Scottish wildlife.

☐ (Tel: Barbreck 653). Open April–September. 15 miles/24 km north of Lochgilphead off A816. OS 55: 79 06.

122 Muirshiel Country Park

Country trail and habitat trail. Woodland with typical flora, birds. Roe Deer. Information Centre. Picnic sites.

☐ Open all year. 3 miles/4.5 km north of Lochwinnoch off B786. OS 63: 31 63.

123 Mull

One of the larger islands offering all the habitats mentioned in the guide. Sea bird colonies on cliffs and over-wintering duck and geese on the sea lochs. Upland areas hold several pairs of Golden Eagles. Natural woodlands are rich in birds, insects and flowers. Information office at Tobermory.

☐ Access to island, car ferry from Oban (A85) or Lochaline (A884). OS 47: 50 55.

124 Paisley Glen Nature Trail

Walk through woodland and streamside habitats. Birds, flowers and fungi.

☐ (Tel: Glasgow 884 37 94). Open all year. Starts at Field Study Unit, Glenfield Road, Glenburn, Paisley off B774. 8 miles/12 km south-west of Glasgow. OS 64: 48 60.

125 Palacerigg Country Park

Woodland walks, birds, Badgers, Foxes, Deer, and small mammals. Paddocks enclosing Mink, Wild Cat, Wolves and other animals. Nature Centre.

☐ Open all year. 2½ miles/4 km south-east of Cumbernauld, north of B803. Off A80 north-east of Glasgow. OS 64: 78 73.

126 Pollok Park

Highland cattle and ponies graze in the park. Two nature trails. One through woodland with rich wildlife and the other a river trail in scenic valley.
☐Trail starts in grounds of Pollok House. (Tel Glasgow 423 8693). Open all year. 3 miles/4.5 km south of Glasgow on A736. OS 64: 54 61.

127 Strathclyde Country Park

Large countryside park bisected by M74. Wide variety of habitats including river, woodland, man-made loch, and meadow.
☐Permit only. Contact the Director, Strathclyde Country Park, 366 Hamilton Road, Motherwell. (Tel: Motherwell 66155). Open July–January. At Hamilton off M74 via A723. OS 64: 72 56.

128 Victoria Park

Gardens include Fossil Grove with famous collection of fossil tree stumps and roots.
☐Open all year. Victoria Park Drive North, opposite Airthrey Avenue, Glasgow. OS 64: 54 67.

129 West Loch Tarbert

An area offering easy viewing of over-wintering duck and geese. Great Northern Diver, Slavonian Grebe, Eider, Velvet Scoter, Barnacle and White-fronted Geese.
☐View from A83 south of Tarbert (several access points) in North Kintyre, or by ferry to islands of Gigha or Islay. OS 62: 84 67.

Central

130 Dollar Glen

National Trust for Scotland. Spectacular steep wooded glen leading to Castle Campbell. Burn-side walks. Woodland plants and birds. Take care as path is narrow and gorge sheer.
☐Open all year. ½ mile/1 km north of Dollar off A91, east of Stirling. OS 58: 96 99.

131 Doune Park Gardens

Gardens including woodland and pinetum with rare conifers dating from 1860s.
☐(Tel: Doune 203). Open April–October.

2 miles/3 km north of Doune off A84. North-west of Stirling. OS 57: 71 03.

132 Flanders Moss

Large area of bog and moor with associated special plant communities and a variety of breeding and over-wintering birds including Hen Harrier, Golden Plover, Curlew, Black Grouse around River Forth. Wildfowl on Lake of Menteith.
☐13 miles/20.5 km west of Stirling between A873 and A811 and, bounded by B8034 and B822. OS 57: 58 01.

133 Keir Gardens

Gardens with trees dating from 1700.
☐(Tel: Dunblane 82 4 00). Open April–October: Tuesday, Wednesday and Thursday afternoons only. 6 miles/9.5 km north of Stirling on A9 off B824. OS 57: 77 99.

134 Mill Glen Nature Trail

Nature trail in steep glen. Botanical and geological interests. Hill walking area. Ranger Service.
☐Upper Mill Street, Tillicoultry. (Tel: Alloa 722160 ext 216). Open all year. East of Stirling on A91. OS 58: 913 980.

135 Queen Elizabeth Forest Park

Forestry Commission. Variety of habitats in an area which extends from Loch Lomond to the Trossachs and includes the summits of Ben Lomond and Ben Venue. Camping and tourist facilities. Forest walks including Loch Lomondside with botanical and winter wildfowl interest, and the Ben Lomond path to summit (3000 ft/900 m) for well-equipped walkers. Fishing.
☐Visitor Centre at David Marshall Lodge open mid-March – mid-October. Off A82, 1½ mile/2 km north of Aberfoyle. North from Glasgow on A81 from Stirling on A873 then A821. OS 57: 52 01.

136 Scotland's Safari Park

Animals include Ankole cattle and Père David deer. Dolphinarium. Children's zoo.
☐(Tel: Doune 456). Open March–October. At Blair Drummond, 6 miles/9.5 km north-west of Stirling off A84. Leave M9 at junction 10. OS 57: 73 98.

Fife

137 Dunfermline Museum

Museum with natural history displays.
☐Viewfield, Dunfermline. (Tel: Dunfermline 21814). Open June–September (except Tuesdays and Sunday mornings); October–May open Wednesday–Sunday only.

138 Eden Estuary

Large numbers of wildfowl and waders (20,000) congregate in this small estuary. Common and Velvet Scoters,Wigeon, Pintail, Eider, Long-tailed Duck, Scaup, Red-breasted Merganser, Oystercatcher, Black-tailed and Bar-tailed Godwits, Curlew. Also migrant route in spring for Little Gull and autumn for Grey Plover, Whimbrel, Spotted Redshank and Ruff.
☐3 miles/4.5 km north-west of St Andrews. OS 59: 50 17.

139 Isle of May National Nature Reserve

Nature Conservancy Council. An important Bird Observatory noted for its passing migrant birds and also sea bird colonies on 150 ft/45 m cliffs – Guillemots, Razorbills, Fulmars, Shags, Kittiwakes, Puffins.
☐(Tel: Kirkcaldy 51587). Open April–October. Island at mouth of Firth of Forth. Access by boat (organized parties only) from Anstruther, 9 miles/14.5 km south of St Andrews. OS 59: inset.

140 Letham Glen Nature Trail

Woodland nature trail, botanical interest.
☐(Tel: Leven 25501). Open all year. 8 miles/12.5 km north-east of Kirkcaldy. OS 59: 38 01.

Lothian

141 Aberlady Bay

Local Nature Reserve. An estuary and sandy bay. Good birdwatching area for autumn migrant waders and for overwintering geese, duck and waders. In winter, the species mainly seen are Pinkfooted Geese, Wigeon, Scoter, Red-breasted Merganser. Long-tailed Duck, Knot, and Red-necked Grebes with a wider range on passage in the autumn and occasional sea duck (Scaup, Goldeneye, Eider) from the Firth of Forth. During the summer there are breeding Dunlin, Redshank, Cormorant, Arctic and Little Terns.
☐20 miles/32 km east of Edinburgh off A198 at Aberlady. OS 66: 47 80.

142 Almondell Country Park

Nature trail and longer walks on ancient drovers' road over Pentland hills. Moorland habitat.
☐10 miles/16 km south-west of Edinburgh off A71 at East Calder. OS 65: 08 67.

143 Bass Rock

Rocky island coast with famous sea bird colonies. Large Gannetry (9000 pairs) on cliffs rising to 350 ft/105 m.
☐Regular trips around island from North Berwick. (Tel: North Berwick 2838). On A198 north-east of Edinburgh. OS 67: 60 87.

144 Beecraigs Country Park

Several walks in variety of woodland and wetland habitats. Information Centre. Fish hatchery. Ranger Service.
☐Open all year. West of Edinburgh junction 3 off M9. South of Linlithgow off A706. OS 65: 00 73.

145 Dalkeith Park

Extensive wooded grounds of Dalkeith Palace. Nature trail, river walks. Orangery.
☐ East of High Street, Dalkeith. Open Easter–October. 7 miles/11 km southeast of Edinburgh off A68. OS 66: 33 67.

146 Hermitage of Braid Nature Trails

Woodland and scrub trails with plant and bird interests close to city. Ranger Service for organized groups.
☐Hermitage Drive, 2 miles/3 km south of Edinburgh. Open all year.

147 Holyrood Park

Surprising variety of wildlife habitats for a city site. Arthur's Seat, a steep grassy hill with some scrub, attracts common town birds and migrants including warblers, Redstart, Tree Pipit and Snow Bunt-

ing. Dunsappie Loch within the park, attracts duck in winter including Wigeon, Mallard, Gadwall, Pochard. Duddingston Loch may be viewed from the park and a wider range of duck and marshland birds observed. Salisbury Crags also within the park is the site of many interesting plant species e g. Red German Catchfly and Forked Spleenwort.
□ On eastern side of Edinburgh city centre next to Holyrood Palace. Leave A1 at Meadow Bank.

148 Hopetoun House and Gardens
A fine example of a Scottish country house. Grounds contain deer parks, nature trail, coastal walk, aviary. Education Centre.
□ (Tel: Edinburgh 331 2451). Open May–September. South Queensferry, off A90 west of Edinburgh. OS 65: 08 79.

149 John Muir Country Park Nature Trail
Cliff-top nature trail of considerable geological, botanical and ornithological interest. Dangerous cliffs: keep to trail.
□ Open all year. East of Edinburgh on A1 to Dunbar Harbour. OS 67: 67 79.

150 Portobello to Musselburgh
Fine views of the Firth of Forth from industrialized area which still attracts large numbers of sea duck in winter including Scaup (up to 30,000 have been recorded), Goldeneye, Scoter, Eider and also Great Crested Grebe.
□ Bus or drive from centre of Edinburgh to Portobello and Musselburgh is to the east. OS 66: 31 73 to 36 73.

151 Pressmennan Forest Trail
Forestry Commission. Trail through Oak, Spruce and Larch plantations. Lake and views to coast.
□ (Tel: Dumfries 2425). Open all year. 6 miles/9.5 km south-west of Dunbar off B6370. OS 67: 62 72.

152 Royal Botanic Gardens
Major centre for identification of botanical specimens in Scotland. Exhibition hall with botanical and horticultural displays.
□ Car park off Arboretum Road in north Edinburgh. Open all year.

153 Scottish National Zoological Park
Displays of mammals, birds and reptiles. Aquarium. Scottish animals. Breeding colony of Penguins. Education Centre.
□ Corstophine Road.(Tel: Edinburgh 334 9171). Open all year. 4 miles/6.5 km west of Edinburgh off A8. OS 66: 20 73.

Borders

154 Dawyck House Gardens
A wooded garden with many rare trees.
□ Open Easter–September daily (afternoons only). 7 miles/11 km south-west of Peebles on A72 then B712. OS 72: 17 35.

155 Duns Castle
Scottish Wildlife Trust. Broadleaved woodland with Beech, Oak, Ash and shrubs of Hazel and Field Maple. Artificial loch with Bogbean and Yellow Water-lily. Woodland birds include Marsh Tit, Pied Flycatcher and Tawny Owl and flowers include Wintergreen and Twayblade.
□ ½ mile/1 km north of Duns, 10 miles/ 16 km west of Berwick-upon-Tweed on A6105. OS 67: 778 550.

156 Hawick Museum
Natural history exhibits in museum. Grounds have river walks.
□ In Wilton Lodge Park, on edge of Hawick, off A7. (Tel: Hawick 3457). Open April–October: daily but afternoons on Sunday; November–March: daily except Sunday. OS 79: 49 14.

157 The Hirsel
Private grounds with woodland and small loch. Scottish birds. Information Centre.
□ The Hirsel, Coldstream. (Tel: Coldstream 2345). Open all year. 2 miles/3 km off A697.

158 St Abb's Head
National Trust for Scotland/Scottish Wildlife Trust. High cliffs 480 ft/145 m extend from St Abb's Head northward to Fast Castle. Sea bird colonies. Rich cliff-top flora. Ranger Service.
□ (Tel: Coldingham 443). 2 miles/3 km north of St Abb's off B6438. OS 67: 91 69.

Dumfries and Galloway

159 Caerlaverock
National Nature Reserve
Nature Conservancy Council. Extensive saltmarsh (locally called merse) between River Nith and the Lochar Water. On the Scottish shore of the Solway Firth. Wintering haunt of wildfowl particularly Barnacle Geese. Also Grey and Pink-footed Geese. Wildfowl Refuge (see Eastpark Farm). Rare Natterjack Toad breeds on the reserve.

☐(Tel: Glencaple 275). Open all year, except sanctuary area. 7 miles/11 km south of Dumfries on B725. OS 84: 01 65.

160 Carse Bay-Southerness Point
Area of estuarine foreshore between Carsethorn village and Southerness lighthouse. Excellent winter birdwatching walk. Scaup seen off Carsethorn; also Greylag, Pink-footed and sometimes Barnacle Geese in nearby fields. Main interest is large number of waders: Knot, Dunlin, Redshank, Oystercatcher, Curlew, Black-tailed and Bar-tailed Godwits. Shelduck, Oystercatcher and Ringed Plover breed.

☐Access via Carsethorn signposted at Kirkbean or at Southerness, both off A710. South of Dumfries. OS 84: 97 59 to 97 54.

161 Devil's Beef Tub
Devil's Beef Tub is a hollow in the Moffat Hills. Moorland vegetation enriched in places by lime-rich outcrops. Fine examples of glacial features (U-shaped valleys, corries). Spectacular gorges, some wooded with rich ground flora.

☐View from A701, 6 miles/9.5 km north of Moffat. OS 78: 06 12.

162 Dumfries Museum
Regional museum with local herbarium and changing displays on local wildlife and history. Best information centre for flora and fauna of Solway Firth area. Local species lists available.

☐The Observatory, Dumfries. (Tel: Dumfries 3374). Open all year. April–September (closed Tuesday); October–March (closed Tuesdays and Sundays).

163 Eastpark Farm
The Wildfowl Trust. Refuge on the Solway Firth includes part of Caerlaverock National Nature Reserve. An observatory, two towers, and hides provide close views of wildfowl and waders. Large numbers of Barnacle Geese, Pink-footed Geese and smaller numbers of Greylag Geese and Golden Plover over-winter. Regular visitors include Bewick's and Whooper Swans, ducks, Oystercatchers, Lapwings, Curlews, Dunlins, Hen Harriers, Peregrine Falcons, and Kestrels.

☐(Tel: Glencaple 200). 7 miles/11 km south of Dumfries on B725. OS 84: 01 65.

164 Fountainbleau and
Ladypark Reserve
Scottish Wildlife Trust. Nature trail through Birchwood reserve. Interest mainly botanical with some bird life.

☐Permit only. Contact the Warden, 25 Rotchell Park, Dumfries. (Tel: Dumfries 3639). Open April–October. Through Dumfries High School playing fields, Marchmont, east of Dumfries.

165 Galloway Forest Park
Forestry Commission. Vast area of Galloway Hills, 16 hill lochs, the highest mountain in southern Scotland (the Merrick) and Rhinns of Kells. Fine views along the A712 from New Galloway to Newton Stewart (Queen's Way) past Red Deer Range, Wild Goat Park and Galloway Deer Museum, with exhibits on wildlife and geology. Several forest walks at Glentrool, signposted off A714 north of Newton Stewart including one around Loch Trool through Oak woodland, Pine and Spruce plantations, and another for hardy and properly equipped walkers to the summit of the Merrick. See also the Merrick. Upland plants and animals. Fishing.

☐10 miles/16 km north-west of Newton Stewart off A714. OS 77: 41 80.

166 Grey Mare's Tail
National Trust for Scotland. Classic example of a glacial hanging valley with high waterfalls. The area has feral Goats, upland birds and notable moorland and cliff vegetation. Part of Moffat Hills. See

also Devil's Beef Tub. Dangerous cliffs: stay on footpaths especially near falls. Ranger Service (summer only).
□10 miles/16 km north-east of Moffat off A708. OS 79: 18 14.

167 Loch Ken/River Dee
Area noted for wetland plant species and large over-wintering congregations of geese (Greylag, Pink-footed and Greenland White-fronted). Whooper Swan, Wigeon, Pintail, Shoveler, Goldeneye, Smew, Gadwall.
□Between Castle Douglas and New Galloway on A713 and A762. OS 84: 73 65.

168 Loch Ryan
Sea duck may be observed from Stranraer and western shore of Loch Ryan during winter. Red-breasted Merganser, Scaup, Eider, Goldeneye, some waders.
□East bank of loch approached from Stranraer via A77. OS 82: 08 62.

169 Logan Botanic Garden
Garden specializes in plants from warm countries. Many rare and tender plants grow here in one of the mildest climates in Scotland.
□Port Logan. (Tel: Stranraer 86231). Open April–September. 14 miles/22.5 km south of Stranraer signposted from A716. OS 82: 09 42.

170 The Merrick
Forestry Commission. Highest mountain (2764 ft/840 m) in the Southern Uplands. Footpath to summit leads from wooded Loch Trool. Moorland plant communities and birds on lower slopes give way to upland and mountain species. Alpine Sawwort, Starry Saxifrage, Mossy Saxifrage, Red Grouse, Raven, Peregrine Falcon, Red Deer and feral Goats. See also Galloway Forest Park.
□12 miles/19 km off A714 north of Newton Stewart signposted to Loch Trool. OS 77: 41 80.

171 Mull of Galloway
RSPB reserve. Most southerly tip of Scotland,notable for cliff-top vegetation close to lighthouse and small sea bird colonies.

□15 miles/24 km south of Stranraer via A716 and B7041, signposted from Drummore. OS 82: 15 30.

172 Threave Gardens and Wildfowl Refuge
National Trust for Scotland. Peat, rock and water gardens in grounds of Threave School of Gardening. Wildfowl Refuge. Opportunities to view over-wintering ducks and geese in Dee Valley. See Loch Ken for species. Visitor Centre.
□(Tel: Castle Douglas 2575). Gardens open all year. Wildfowl Refuge open November–March only. Keep to access points. 2 miles/3 km west of Castle Douglas. OS 84: 75 60.

173 Wigtown Bay
The bay in the estuary of the River Cree, attracts several thousand Pink-footed and Greylag Geese in winter and many duck and wader species. Wigeon, Mallard, Teal, Pintail, Shoveler, Shelduck, Curlew and Oystercatcher. Extensive saltmarsh contains typical plant communities and unusual fossil shell beds.
□Access from minor roads off A746 south of Wigtown. Access restricted, long walks often necessary to reach vantage points. OS 83: 43 55.

174 Wigtown Moors
Moorland with vegetation typical of large areas of lowland Wigtownshire. Much of this habitat is now planted with conifers but extensive tracts remain with characteristic bog and moorland plants and animals.
□May be viewed from A75 between Newton Stewart and Glenluce or alongside minor road from B7027 north of Newton Stewart to Glenluce. OS 82: 27 65.

175 Wood of Cree
Forestry Commission. An ancient coppiced Oakwood on the valley slopes of the River Cree. Woodland plants and birds to east of road; scrub and bog alongside the river on the west side, with Alder woods.
□4 miles/6.5 km north of Newton Stewart on minor road off A75 at Minnigaff. OS 77: 385 710.

Conservation

Britain still offers a variety of habitats rich in wildlife, and areas of wild and beautiful countryside; but these areas are threatened as more land is taken up by industry, housing and agriculture.

When hedgerows are removed and woodlands are cleared, wetlands drained, heaths replaced by forestry plantations, and trees felled indiscriminately, vital habitats are destroyed. The aim of wildlife conservation is to preserve existing habitats and manage them so as to ensure that the species dependent upon these habitats survive.

In Britain the official organization for the conservation of wildlife is the Nature Conservancy Council. They seek to inform farmers, planners and industrialists about environmental problems and to gain their co-operation in caring for the environment. The Council also protects important habitats by setting aside certain areas as nature reserves.

The ultimate responsibility for the survival of our wildlife lies with everyone, if the variety of countryside and wildlife is to remain and be enjoyed by future generations. The Countryside Commission has drawn up guidelines for visitors to the countryside. The main points are listed below.

The Country Code

Guard against all risk of fire.
Fasten all gates.
Keep dogs under proper control.
Keep to the paths across farm land.
Avoid damaging fences, hedges, walls.
Leave no litter.
Safeguard water supplies.
Protect wildlife, wild plants and trees.
Go carefully on country roads.
Respect the life of the countryside.

● *The Conservation of Wild Creatures and Wild Plants Act* makes it illegal to pick certain plants which are so rare as to be endangered, and to uproot *any wild plant* without the landowner's permission.

● *The Bird Protection Act* makes it illegal to take the eggs or disturb any wild bird at its nest.

Nature Conservation in Scotland

Though Scotland still boasts great expanses of unspoilt countryside and comparatively low density of people, much of the landscape is modified by man. Further modifications that permanently alter wildlife habitats continue to take place and present a serious threat to Scotland's animals and plants.

Much of the native forest of Scotland has been cleared to make way for farming. Peatlands with their bogs and moors disappear as they are drained and afforested with non-native conifers. Extensive coastlands, once the rich feeding grounds for thousands of water birds, have been reclaimed for industrial development. Oil pollution from ships and industry pollutes beaches and kills thousands of birds each year. Even human access to areas of wilderness presents a threat to the wildlife that thrives in undisturbed places.

To combat these threats action is being taken: the RSPB, the Scottish Wildlife Trust and the Nature Conservancy Council own and lease nature reserves; universities and government research stations are studying the environmental impact of large-scale changes in land use such as afforestation; and steps are being taken to control oil pollution.

Greater co-operation between organizations concerned with agriculture, forestry, industry recreation and nature conservation will however be necessary to ensure that future developments to utilize Scotland's natural resources will also safeguard its wildlife heritage.

Scots Pine, a native conifer. Scots Pine woods once covered extensive areas of the Highlands of Scotland but, since large tracts have been destroyed by man, they are now restricted to a few glens. Efforts are being made to conserve the character of the few remaining areas of native woodland.

Hill Safety

The weather conditions in Britain's hills and mountains, always unreliable and colder than in the valleys, are still more changeable and more severe in Scotland than in England and Wales. In Scotland even in summer, snow or sleet blizzards may occur at altitudes above 800 metres (2500 feet). Gale force winds are also frequent in the mountains, increasing the risk of exposure and exhaustion.

It is always advisable when going walking in hills and mountains to be well-prepared and be reasonably careful. Here are some guidelines:

● Don't be over-ambitious when planning walks, especially with children.

● Take note of weather forecasts and local information Notice Boards before setting off. Be prepared to change your route or turn back if the weather turns bad.

● Leave word with someone before setting off of where you intend to walk and how long you expect to be out.

● Wear or take with you warm clothing, including windproof and waterproof outer clothing, and headgear and gloves. Wear boots rather than shoes and never wear smooth soles, especially not smooth-soled rubber boots.

● A rucksack leaves your hands free for scrambling up and down steeper slopes.

Carry the following items:

Good maps, preferably Ordnance Survey maps.

A survival bag or tent for shelter.

A compass: in misty conditions, using a compass may be the only means of finding your way down.

Food such as chocolate and glucose sweets.

Basic first aid kit such as elastoplast, lint, antiseptic, crepe bandage.

An accurate watch.

A torch.

A whistle.

● Avoid crossing streams, for even shallow ones can swell after rain and make crossing them on return impossible, especially when peat-staining makes the depth of the water difficult to judge.

● Avoid treading on scree or loose rock.

● In an emergency, six flashes of a torch or six blasts on a whistle is the signal that you need help.

Further Reading

Highland Animals. David Stephen (Highlands and Islands Development Board: 1974)

Highland Birds. Desmond Nethersole-Thompson (Highland and Islands Development Board: 1974)

Highland Flora. Derek Ratcliffe (Highlands and Islands Development Board: 1977)

The Highlands and Islands. F. F. Darling & J. M. Boyd (Collins: 1964)

Explore the Highlands and Islands. Alan Campbell McLean (Highlands and Islands Development Board: 1977)

Geology and Scenery in Scotland. J. B. Whittow (Penguin: 1977)

Scottish Highlands. W. H. Murray (Scottish Mountaineering Trust: 1976)

Scotland for Hillwalking. Scottish Tourist Board (1978)

Walks and Trails in Scotland. Scottish Tourist Board (1978)

Wildlife of Scotland. Fred Holliday (ed) (Macmillan: 1979)

The Birds of Britain and Europe. Heinzel, Fitter and Parslow (Collins: 1972)

Where to Watch Birds. John Gooders (Pan: 1974)

A Field Guide to the Mammals of Britain and Europe. F. H. Van den Brink (Collins: 1973)

A Field Guide to the Trees of Britain and Northern Europe. Alan Mitchell (Collins: 1974)

Finding Wild Flowers. R. S. R. Fitter (Collins: 1971)

The Wildflowers of Britain and Northern Europe. Fitter, Fitter and Blamey (Collins: 1971)

Hamlyn Guide to the Seashore and Shallow Seas of Britain and Europe. A. C. Campbell (Hamlyn: 1976)

Mountains and Moorlands. W. H. Pearsall (Collins: 1974)

Useful Addresses

Botanical Society of the British Isles
c/o Natural History Museum, Cromwell Road, London SW7. Concerned with the distribution of flowering plants and ferns of Britain. Has a network of recorders, organizes field meetings and publishes books and guides.

The Countryside Commission for Scotland
Battleby House, Redgorton, Perth PH1 3EW. Concerned with the development and improvement of facilities for enjoyment of the countryside. Publishes guide to Scotland's countryside.

Forestry Commission
Information Offices, 231 Corstorphine Road, Edinburgh. State Forestry authority which manages national forests in Britain. Publishes guides to forest walks, nature trails and recreational facilities on their land.
Regional Offices:
East Scotland Region: 6 Queen's Gate, Aberdeen
North Scotland Region: 21 Church Street, Inverness
South Scotland Region: Greystone Park, 55/57 Moffat Road, Dumfries
West Scotland Region: Portcullis House, 21 Indian Street, Glasgow

Scottish Field Studies Association,
(Kindrogan Field Centre)
Enochdhu, Blairgowrie, Tayside. Important centre for the study of wildlife in Scotland. Residential courses on botany, ornithology, geology, mammals, wildlife photography, run by leading naturalists. Write for details.

Nature Conservancy Council
12 Hope Terrace, Edinburgh. Government body responsible for nature conservation throughout Britain. Safeguards sites and species and offers advice on conservation issues to all whose activity affects the countryside. Publishes guides on national nature reserves and series of pamphlets on conservation topics.

Regional Offices:
North-East Region: Wynne-Edwards House, 17 Rubislaw Terrace, Aberdeen
North-West Region: Fraser Darling House, 9 Culduthel Road, Inverness
South-East Region: 12 Hope Terrace, Edinburgh
South-West Region: The Castle, Loch Lomond Park, Balloch, Dunbartonshire

National Trust for Scotland
5 Charlotte Square, Edinburgh. Preserves places of historical, architectural and landscape interest. Publishes guide to Trust properties and Ranger/Naturalist services.

RSPB (Royal Society for the Protection of Birds)
17 Regent Terrace, Edinburgh. Voluntary organization for encouragement and conservation of wildlife. Manages nature reserves and organizes educational and interpretation facilities.

Scottish Ornithologists' Club
21 Regent Terrace, Edinburgh. Encourages and directs study of Scottish birds and protection of rare species. Official recorders throughout Scotland. Publishers journal, organizes lectures and excursions and puts out annual bird report. Ornithological information from Scottish Centre for Ornithology and Bird Protection at same address.

Scottish Tourist Board
23 Ravelston Terrace, Edinburgh. Promotes tourist facilities in Scotland. Organizes network of information offices and publishes holiday guide, accommodation list, maps.

Scottish Wildlife Trust
8 Dublin Street, Edinburgh. Voluntary organization for conservation of wildlife in Scotland. Manages nature reserves, offers advice on countryside issues and conducts scientific survey. Publishes journal on its reserves and nature trails.

Index

Page numbers in bold refer to illustrations. Place names appearing in "Places to Visit" are generally listed under the appropriate category (eg. nature reserves, zoos, country parks). Only certain bird species mentioned in the "Places to Visit" section have been indexed. Those included in the index are either relatively rare or restricted to a few sites, or provide the main interest of the particular entry.

Acknowledgements:
Photographers and Artists

Photographs and paintings are credited by page, from left to right running down page.

Cover: R. T. Smith, H. Kinloch/Aquila, Geoffrey Kinns, Geoffrey Kinns, John Mason, (painting) Phil Weare/Linden Artists, John Woolverton. *Back cover*: John Sibbick/John Martin Artists.

Page 1: B. S. Turner. *Page 3*: B. S. Turner. *Pages 4–7* (maps): Swanston Associates. *Page 8*: R. H. Bridson. *Page 9*: R. H. Bridson. *Page 10*: Scottish Tourist Board. *Page 11*: Geoffrey Kinns, B. S. Turner, E. O. Fellowes, J. Roberts/Aquila, H. Kinloch/Aquila, R. H. Bridson, Roger Beecroft, J. Good/NHPA. *Page 13*: J. F. Young, B. S. Turner, Geoffrey Kinns, B. S. Turner, R. H. Bridson, Scottish Tourist Board. *Page 14*: E. O. Fellowes, R. H. Bridson, R. H. Bridson, R. H. Bridson, R. H. Bridson, R. H. Bridson, B. Kinloch. *Page 15*: G. Nystrand, B. S. Turner. *Page 16*: E. O. Fellowes, J. F. Young, R. H. Bridson. *Page 17*: D. Dalton/NHPA, E. O. Fellowes, B. S. Turner, E. O. Fellowes, R. T. Smith, E. O. Fellowes, J. F. Young, J. F. Young. *Page 18*: Geoffrey Kinns, R. V. Collier, B. S. Turner, R. H. Bridson, Heather Angel, M. C. F. Proctor, R. H. Bridson. *Page 19*: J. F. Young, Scottish Tourist Board, R. H. Bridson. *Page 20*: B. S. Turner, E. O. Fellowes, B. S. Turner. *Page 21*: B. S. Turner, M. Wright, B. Kinloch, B. S. Turner, John Mason, (painting) Victoria Goaman. *Page 22*: P. Scott/NHPA, R. T. Smith, R. H. Bridson, R. H. Bridson, J. F. Young, B. Kinloch. *Page 23*: M. Savories/NHPA, Heather Angel, D. Chesterman, Heather Angel. *Page 24*: R. Mearns. *Page 25*: R. Mearns, B. S. Turner, R. T. Smith, R. Mearns, B. S. Turner. *Page 26*: B. S. Turner, R. H. Bridson, P. Scott/NHPA, W. S. Paton/Aquila, R. Mearns, R. H. Bridson. *Page 27*: R. Mearns, J. F. Young, B. Kinloch, R. H. Bridson, J. F. Young. *Page 28*: Geoffrey Kinns, T. Andrewartha/Aquila, Geoffrey Kinns, J. F. Young, B. S. Turner, B. S. Turner. *Page 29*: J. F. Young, B. S. Turner, B. S. Turner, B. S. Turner, J. F. Young, J. F. Young, G. Bates/Aquila, R. T. Smith. *Page 30*: John Mason, J. F. Young, R. T. Smith, M. C. F. Proctor, M. J. Woods. *Page 31*: (painting) John Sibbick/John Martin Artists. *Page 32*: R. T. Smith, B. S. Turner, John Mason, M. J. Woods, I. C. Rose, Mark Wilson. *Page 33*: John Sibbick. *Pages 34–53*: Trevor Boyer. *Page 54*: Chris Shields/Wilcock Riley. *Page 55*: David Wright/Tudor Art, Chris Shields/Wilcock Riley. *Page 56*: Chris Shields/Wilcock Riley. *Pages 57–70*: Hilary Burn. *Page 71*: Hilary Burn, Michelle Emblem/Middletons, Hilary Burn. *Pages 72–8*: Hilary Burn. *Pages 79–80*: Joyce Bee. *Page 81*: Joyce Bee, Chris Shields/Wilcock Riley. *Page 82*: Joyce Bee. *Pages 83–5*: John Barber. *Page 86*: John Barber, Michelle Emblem/Middletons. *Pages 87–8*: John Barber. *Pages 89–95*: Annabel Milne & Peter Stebbing. *Page 96*: Annabel Milne & Peter Stebbing, Bob Bampton/Garden Studio (Hawthorn). *Page 97*: Heather Angel. Maps on pages 98–101: Swanston Associates. *Page 121*: Victoria Goaman.